SUPPORTING
YOUNG PARENTS

of related interest

Kids Need...
Parenting Cards for Families and the People who Work with Them
Mark Hamer
ISBN 978 1 84310 524 4 (Card Game)

Kinship Care
Fostering Effective Family and Friends Placements
Elaine Farmer and Sue Moyers
ISBN 978 1 84310 631 9
Quality Matters in Children's Services series

Passionate Supervision
Edited by Robin Shohet
ISBN 978 1 84310 556 5

Professional Risk and Working with People
Decision-Making in Health, Social Care and Criminal Justice
David Carson and Andy Bain
ISBN 978 1 84310 389 9

Residential Child Care
Prospects and Challenges
Edited by Andrew Kendrick
ISBN 978 1 84310 526 8
Research Highlights in Social Work series

Young People's Transitions from Care to Adulthood
International Research and Practice
Edited by Mike Stein and Emily R. Munro
ISBN 978 1 84310 610 4
Child Welfare Outcomes series

Babies and Young Children in Care
Life Pathways, Decision-making and Practice
Harriet Ward, Emily R. Munro and Chris Dearden
ISBN 978 1 84310 272 4
Child Welfare Outcomes series

SUPPORTING
YOUNG PARENTS

Pregnancy and Parenthood among Young People from Care

Elaine Chase, Ian Warwick, Abigail Knight, and Peter Aggleton

Foreword by Ann Phoenix

Jessica Kingsley Publishers
London and Philadelphia

First published in 2009
by Jessica Kingsley Publishers
116 Pentonville Road
London N1 9JB, UK
and
400 Market Street, Suite 400
Philadelphia, PA 19106, USA

www.jkp.com

Copyright © Elaine Chase, Ian Warwick, Abigail Knight and Peter Aggleton 2009
Foreword copyright © Ann Phoenix 2009

Library of Congress Cataloging in Publication Data
Supporting young parents : pregnancy and parenthood among young people from care /
Elaine Chase ... [et al.].
    p. cm.
Includes bibliographical references and index.
ISBN 978-1-84310-525-1 (pb : alk. paper) 1. Teenage parents. 2. Teenage parents--Counseling of. 3. Teenage parents--Services for. 4. Teenage pregnancy. 5. Home-based family services. I. Chase, Elaine, 1962-
    HQ759.64.S87 2009
    362.820835--dc22

                                2008023390

British Library Cataloguing in Publication Data
A CIP catalogue record for this book is available from the British Library

ISBN 9781843105251

Printed and bound in Great Britain by
Athenaeum Press, Gateshead, Tyne and Wear

CONTENTS

ACKNOWLEDGEMENTS 7
FOREWORD BY ANN PHOENIX 9

1 Introduction 13

2 Putting Pregnancy and Parenthood in Context 37

3 Being Young, Being in Care 55

4 Going It Alone: Young People's Experiences of
Learning about Sex and Relationships 70

5 Deciding What to Do: Young People's Reactions and
Responses to Pregnancy 85

6 Being Pregnant 102

7 Being a Mum, Being a Dad 121

8 Finding a Balance: Young People's Experiences of
Child Protection Proceedings 138

9 Getting Help from Services 151

10 Moving Forward 167

REFERENCES 178
SUBJECT INDEX 185
AUTHOR INDEX 190

Dedication

In memory of Kim Rivers, a dear friend and colleague, who started the project on teenage pregnancy among young people in care, of which this book is the culmination. Her dedication to research and writing, and her wonderful sense of humour, inspire our work and won't be forgotten.

ACKNOWLEDGEMENTS

The research on which this book is based was conducted at the Thomas Coram Research Unit at the Institute of Education, University of London. It was funded by the Department of Health, to which we express our sincere thanks. The views expressed throughout the book, however, belong to the authors and the young people participating in our study.

We would like especially to thank all the young people who participated and who were so willing to share their lives and experiences with us. Thanks also go to the many professionals and carers across the various study sites who gave generously of their time and commitment.

We thank also the various members of the research team who worked with us on the study: Maria Zuurmond, Lisa Ruxton, Ekua Yankah, Sarah Heathcote, Claire Maxwell and Stuart Watson. In addition, special thanks go to Antonia Simon and Charlie Owen, who provided statistical expertise and knowledge to the project, and to Penny Mellor, who provided invaluable administrative support throughout.

Our thanks also go to all the members of the specialist advisory group for support and guidance: Carolyn Davies, Sharmila Kaduskar, Catherine Dennison, Lisa Williams (all at the Department of Health); Helen Jones (Department for Education and Skills); Mark Jennet and Geraldine McCormack (Health Development Agency); Helen Chambers and Gill Frances (National Children's Bureau); Sarah Carter (Buckinghamshire Health Authority); Caroline Thomas (University of Stirling); Emma Beckwith (A National Voice); Janet Janeway (Swindon Borough Council); Nigel Farrow (Nottingham Social Services

Department); Christine Humphrey (Social Services Inspectorate, Quality Protects); Roger Ingham (Centre for Sexual Health Research, University of Southampton); Melvyn Davis (Coram Family); and Judith Corlyon (Tavistock Institute).

For the book as a whole, special thanks go to Daisy Ellis for her administrative support.

FOREWORD

Young people who have been 'looked after' by local authorities are more likely than their peers to become parents while they are teenagers. In a context where teenage parenting and outcomes for those leaving care are both the subject of policy intervention, it might be expected that they will have been the focus of a great deal of research. Yet, we know relatively little about the lives and perspectives of young parents who have been looked after.

This book helps to advance understanding of the experiences of this group of young parents and, in doing so, gives practical insights into ways in which they might be supported. Its major contribution results from the careful, contextualised research it reports on, its nuanced attention to what young parents say and its non-moralising and non-pathologising stance. The authors are to be commended for managing to include young fathers in the study (rather than only young mothers, as is more common). They are thus able to analyse both mothers' and fathers' feelings about, and experiences of, young parenthood and, in some cases, to juxtapose what each member of a parental couple say about pregnancy, parenting and their relationships.

The introductory chapter contextualises contemporary perspectives on young people, pregnancy, parenthood and support for those looked after by situating them historically and within current legislation. It presents simple summaries of the government policies and programmes that aim both to safeguard children and to promote their well-being. This in itself would constitute a valuable resource for those working with or researching young parents and/or those looked after. However, this book does much more.

From Chapter 2 onwards, the authors bring alive the members of their sample by examining what they say and contextualising their accounts in their personal histories, the experiences of the sample as a whole and the wider social context. These detailed accounts allow readers to become familiar with the circumstances of the young people's lives and make it easy to understand where the policy messages presented come from and why they are relevant. It is worth highlighting some of the main messages that unfold in the chapters that follow. By definition all the young people had disrupted family relationships, but they also commonly report experiences of inadequate sex education and lack of adult attention to the early, and often unsatisfactory, initiation of their sexual careers. On leaving care, many had difficulty obtaining high quality accommodation. Although they shared such problematic experiences, the young people were differentiated by ethnicity, the numbers of children they have, the age at which they first had them and their familial and relationship histories. As a result, the impact of parenthood and how they were able to deal with it also differed.

The chapters that follow do not romanticise the young people's lives. For example, we meet a couple whose three children have been removed because of their heroin use and see their disappointment with the rudimentary help they received in dealing with their dependency. In contrast, we also meet a mother who is helped, when pregnant, by the mother of her violent partner and taken into a refuge. We see a mother striving to get appropriate help so that she can give her two children, who have disabilities, the best possible life.

Yet, despite the difficulties they faced, the young people are mostly positive about their experiences of being pregnant and of parenthood. Many talk of the new responsibilities that parenthood entails, but most welcome the stability that children brought to lives previously much disrupted. They express commitment to their children and determination to give them the security they themselves lacked in childhood. When we meet them in the early years of their children's lives, they were making strenuous efforts to do so, despite the difficult circumstances many faced.

Their love for their children and satisfaction with parenthood are poignantly tangible in their accounts.

The research findings presented in this book challenge the notion that disadvantaged young people necessarily have low expectations for the future. However, as the authors make clear, how the young people and their children fare is partly dependent on the support they receive from a range of different agencies. The book is invaluable in providing vivid illustrations of the strengths and needs of young parents who have been looked after and, therefore, of their children at the start of their lives. It illuminates policy and practice implications and points the way forward to what needs to be done to ameliorate their lives. Throughout, it presents its research in an accessible style and measured tone that make it difficult to put down. I hope that the careful evaluation of the findings in relation to current legislation and policy will provide the impetus for the re-evaluation of what would constitute adequate support for young parents who have been looked after and for their children.

Ann Phoenix
Co-Director of the Thomas Coram Research Unit,
Institute of Education, University of London

CHAPTER 1

INTRODUCTION

YOUNG PEOPLE

Ask people what they think about 'adolescents' or 'teenagers' and they may say a number of things. Ask about young people in care, and again a certain image is likely to emerge. Ask about teenage parents and the picture is often clear.

Adolescents are said by some to be moody and insecure, perhaps aggressive, impulsive, reckless and rebellious – or even awkward, clumsy and overly impressionable (Young 2008). Young people in care may be said to be troubled and troublesome, possibly ignorant and with a tendency to delinquency (Home Office 2004). In many people's minds, teenage parents are either feckless or sexually irresponsible young mothers who hold a desire to secure, unfairly, social housing or benefits, while teenage fathers are more than likely to be absent from their children's care (Sawtell *et al.* 2005).

These contemporary, yet unhelpful, views can be seen to have particular roots. Over one hundred years ago, for example, G. Stanley Hall's book, *Adolescence: Its Psychology and its Relations to Physiology, Anthropology, Sociology, Sex, Crime, Religion and Education* linked young people's lives to negative and problematic characteristics (Hall 1904). The 1950s brought us the 'teenager' together with adult anxieties about the development of distinctive youthful lifestyles and cultures (Abrams 1959). With the increasing commercialisation of young people's lives in the 1960s and 1970s came concerns about the impact of consumption on the morals, manners and countercultures of young people (Davis 1990).

By the 1980s, youth unemployment alongside concerns about youth crime contributed to a renewed focus on the supervision and management of young people's lives so as to encourage individual responsibility and orderliness (France 2007). Now, at the start of a new millennium, young people in the UK and elsewhere continue to be vilified as wayward, hedonistic and irresponsible, particularly with respect to alcohol, sex and violence (Miller *et al.* 2007; Szmigin *et al.* 2008; Ward 2008).

Increasingly, however, ideas that stigmatise, stereotype or marginalise young people are being moderated by those that seek to 'pay at least as much attention to the development of competences, resources, skills, and assets as to…disadvantage and risk' (Schoon and Bynner 2003, p.21). Among policy makers and practitioners, there is increasing interest in protective factors (the circumstances that moderate the effects of risk), as well as resilience (the positive adaptation in the face of adversities), that can shape young people's lives (Gilligan 2000; National Chilren's Homes (NCH) 2007; O'Dougherty Wright and Marsten 2006; Rutter 1999).

However, even if we think of young people in more positive terms, we should also keep in mind that they are not all the same. While there may be commonalities among young people, there are important differences too – with these shaped as much by social and cultural as they are by individual factors. During the 1960s, 'dropping out' of school, for example, required a degree of material resources and so could be afforded by some more than others (Brake 1985). During the 1980s (and beyond), young people from Black and minority ethnic communities appeared to be particularly disadvantaged during periods of high unemployment (France 2007; Gilroy 1987). In that decade, too, efforts were made to normalise and institutionalise heterosexuality through prohibiting the 'promotion' of same sex relationships (Carabine 1996). Moreover, young women with children were the focus, in particular, of media attention that stigmatised them as mothers and suggested that many had become parents only to secure social housing (Carabine 1996; Daguerre and Nativel 2006).

Ideas like these can alert us to the role that wider social factors play in young people's lives, 'even resilient young people who show high competences and aspirations despite experiencing socioeconomic disadvantage do not succeed to the same extent as young people from more privileged backgrounds' (Schoon and Bynner 2003, p.26). Young people can encounter circumstances that present them with problems which, although not insurmountable, may restrict their ability to make the most of opportunities. These wider social factors require a paradigm shift in health-related practice, policies and programmes, away from positioning some young people as the problem and towards addressing the adverse circumstances that limit the potential of certain young people.

Since the late 1990s, a number of government policies and programmes have gone some way in seeking to safeguard and support young people's physical, emotional, intellectual, social and economic well-being. *Every Child Matters* (Department for Education and Skills (DfES) 2004), the Children Act 2004, *Youth Matters* (DfES 2005b), the *National Service Framework for Children, Young People and Maternity Services* (Department of Health (DH) 2004), the *National Teenage Pregnancy Strategy* (Social Exclusion Unit 1999a), *Teenage Pregnancy: Accelerating the Strategy to 2010* (DfES 2006a), the Children (Leaving Care) Act 2000, the *Care Matters: Transforming the Lives of Children and Young People* Green Paper (DfES 2006b), the *Care Matters: Time for Change* White Paper (DfES 2007) and the *Children's Plan: Building Brighter Futures* (Department for Children, Schools and Families (DCSF) 2007b) all offer frameworks at the national level in England to ensure that local authorities and primary care trusts can better support children and young people in general and assist those facing challenging circumstances in particular.

Every Child Matters, for example, seeks to ensure that all children and young people enjoy good physical and mental health and live a healthy lifestyle, that they stay safe and are protected from harm and neglect, that they get the most out of life and develop the skills needed for adulthood, that they are involved in and with communities and do not engage in antisocial or offending behaviour, and that they are not prevented by economic disadvantage from achieving their full potential in life. The Children Act 2004 offers the legislative backbone to *Every Child Matters*, and the *National Service Framework for Children, Young People and Maternity Services* outlines a ten-year strategy to promote the health and well-being of children and young people which takes account of their individual needs and circumstances through strengthening the integration of health, social care and education services.

Teenage Pregnancy: Accelerating the Strategy to 2010 (DfES 2006a) aims, among other things, to enhance the quality of the lives of teenage parents by improving access to contraception to reduce repeat or unplanned pregnancies, provide more and better quality health, housing and support services and assist young parents back into education, employment or training.

Most recently, the *Children's Plan: Building Brighter Futures* (DCSF, 2007b) provides the government's ten-year strategy to secure the well-being of children and young people, safeguard the young and vulnerable, promote excellence and equity in terms of educational achievement (particularly for those most disadvantaged), ensure that young people achieve their potential to 18 years and beyond, and keep children and young people on the path to success. It is envisaged that the strategy will be achieved through system-wide reforms to the way that services for children and young people work together.

YOUNG PEOPLE, PREGNANCY AND PARENTHOOD

The fact that England has one of the highest rates of teenage conceptions for young women under the age of 18 years is now widely known (Bradshaw 2006; Cheesbrough, Ingham and Massey 1999; Social Exclusion Unit 1999a). Around three-quarters of mothers under the age of 20 years report that their pregnancies are unplanned (Social Exclusion Unit 1999a) and young women tend to make it known that they are pregnant at a later stage than older women, perhaps as a result of a lack of awareness, denial or fear of the anger of others (Social Exclusion Unit 1999a). Although perhaps unplanned, many of the babies born to teenage mothers are nonetheless wanted (Aggleton, Oliver and Rivers 1998; Alan Guttmacher Institute 1998).

In 1999, the National Teenage Pregnancy Strategy was launched in England (Social Exclusion Unit 1999a). At that time, the national under-18 conception rate for England was 46.6 per 1000. The goals of the strategy were to halve the conception rate among young people aged 18 and under by 2010 and to reduce the long-term exclusion of teenage parents through the provision of support so that they could access education, training and employment. The goals were to be met through a national campaign which included clear messages about sex and pregnancy, improved education about sex and relationships and better access to contraceptive services, 'joined-up' action at national level – through an inter-ministerial task force – and at local level – through a teenage pregnancy partnership board coordinated by a local teenage pregnancy coordinator – and greater assistance for young parents through the provision of support services including education, work opportunities, childcare provision and housing. The strategy signalled an important policy shift away from viewing teenage pregnancy as an issue of illegitimacy and welfare dependency (the mark of earlier Conservative government policies) towards one of public health, social exclusion and health inequalities (Acheson 1998; Daguerre 2006).

Despite an overall 10 per cent decrease in the national under-18 conception rate since the national Teenage Pregnancy Strategy was published (DfES 2005a), this downturn has not been seen across all parts of England. Furthermore, within local authorities, social and geographical variations in conception rates are frequently reported. Subsequent government guidance has therefore emphasised the need to target programmes and interventions at the most vulnerable young people and those living in neighbourhoods where there is a high conception rate (DfES 2005a).

More recent research conducted by the government's Teenage Pregnancy Unit (DfES, 2006a) has identified a range of factors that appear to enable a reduction in teenage pregnancy in identifiable 'hot spot' areas – that is, in those areas (defined by electoral wards) where the teenage conception rates are higher than in the local authority as a whole. This research indicated that a local teenage pregnancy strategy was most likely to be successful when a number of conditions were fulfilled: all key partner agencies contributed to the strategy; a local 'champion' provided clear leadership for the work; there was strong delivery of sex and relationships education and workforce training to enhance the quality of sex and relationships education; the existence of accessible, confidential and well-known sexual health services; effective outreach work; effective service referral for 'at risk groups', and where there was an active and well-resourced youth service.

In 2006, the government published *Teenage Pregnancy: Accelerating the Strategy to 2010* (DfES 2006a), outlining its vision of how best to consolidate the success of the strategy since 1999 and further focusing support in areas where teenage pregnancy rates continue to increase or fail to decline. While advocating preventive initiatives tailored to specific geographical 'neighbourhoods' or 'hot spot' areas with persistently high teenage pregnancy rates, this document also acknowledged that some young people may be more at risk of early pregnancy and parenthood as a result of a combination of factors over and beyond where they live. The strategy, therefore, encouraged an additional focus on 'vulnerable groups' of young people. These include those who are sexually active at a young age, those who have identifiable mental health problems, those using alcohol and/or drugs, those who are already teenage parents or whose parents were teenage parents themselves, young people in or leaving public care and those who are disengaged from education or leave school with no qualifications. As such, this stage of the national strategy encourages a more nuanced and sophisticated analysis of the individual as well as economic and social factors that may increase the likelihood of early pregnancy and parenthood for some young people.

YOUNG PEOPLE'S KNOWLEDGE AND ATTITUDES ABOUT SEX

Across the world, the age at which young women and men first have sex varies quite considerably (Alan Guttmacher Institute 1998; Daguerre 2006; Social Exclusion Unit 1999a). Such variation may, in part, relate to different societal contexts, cultures and expectations with respect to sex and expressions of sexuality. It is also indicative of young people's own knowledge, attitudes and values about sex and their skills or ability to have sex when ready and without regret (Wellings *et al.* 2001; Wight *et al.* 2000). A number of broad social factors, as well as those more local and even individual in nature, affect whether and why young women and young men have sex, whether young women become pregnant, and whether young people then go on to become a teenage mother or father.

For young people to extend and enhance their knowledge about sex and sexuality requires not only that they have access to correct guidance and information but also that they are provided with opportunities to

correct what have been reported to be significant levels of misinforma-
tion (Chambers, Wakley and Chambers 2001; DH 2001a; Lindsay,
Smith and Rosenthal 1999). Young people can receive accurate as well as
confusing or misleading messages about sex from a number of sources –
the mass media, for example, as well as teachers, parents and friends. In
particular, young people have been reported to value the media as a
source of information about sex and relationships. Given that the media
at once promote and disapprove of youthful sexuality, it is important to
assist young people to think and respond critically to what they see and
hear (Daves 1995; Scottish Executive 2000) and to provide opportunities for them to clarify their feelings and develop their personal and communication skills (Card 1999; Health Development Agency 2001).

Education about relationships and sex in schools in England aims to
engage with young people's attitudes and values, their knowledge and
understanding and their personal and social skills (Department for Education and Employment (DfEE) 2000). School-based education about
relationships and sex has the potential to reach almost all young people
attending school under 16 and, as part of a broader programme of
personal, social, health and citizenship education, to utilise links
between school and local sexual health services and to promote partner-
ships with parents (Burtney 2000).

An increasing focus in government policy on addressing issues of
young people's knowledge, attitudes and experiences of sex, sexuality
and sexual well-being has prompted unfounded concerns (Kirby 1999;
Kirby, Laris and Rolleri 2007; Mueller, Gavin and Kulkarni 2008;
Wellings et al. 1995; Wellings et al. 2001) among more conservative
circles that sex education might encourage early sexual activity among
young people. Calls have even been made to limit sex education to the
promotion of abstinence only (Blake and Francis 2001). A more widely
held concern, however, is that sex education has not gone far enough and
has had limited efficacy in reducing early pregnancy (Wight et al. 2002).
Young people, for example, are often reported to describe sex education
as 'too little, too late' (Buston and Wight 2002, 2006).

Generally speaking, however, the more comprehensive the
programme of sexual health promotion and education, the more effective
it appears to be in supporting safer sexual knowledge, attitudes and

behaviour among young people (Collins *et al.* 2002; Ray 1998). Those countries with lower rates of teenage conception than in England typically share a number of characteristics: they provide education about sex and relationships in schools, enable access to contraception and confidential sexual health services, support familial and societal discussion regarding sex and have a generally positive and pragmatic attitude towards young people's sexuality (Daguerre and Nativel 2006; UNICEF 2001; Wellings *et al.* 2001).

YOUNG PEOPLE'S USE OF CONTRACEPTION

These wider societal views of young people's sexuality create the context within which young people make decisions about their access to and use of contraceptive methods. Contexts such as the USA and to some extent the UK, where there is an element of shame and secrecy surrounding young people having sex, contrast starkly with countries like Sweden, Norway and Denmark, which have developed dedicated contraceptive services for young people since the 1970s alongside more comprehensive sex education policies (Daguerre and Nativel 2006; UNICEF 2001).

The proportion of young people who use contraception at first intercourse varies between countries. While in the Netherlands, for example, 85 per cent of young people reported using some form of contraception the first time they had sex, in the UK as a whole, 66 per cent of 16–19 year olds (and 50 per cent of under 16s) reported doing so (Social Exclusion Unit 1999a). The inconsistent or incorrect use of contraceptives by young people has proved to be as important a cause of pregnancy as the failure of young people to use them (Burghes and Brown 1995; Keirnan 1995; Social Exclusion Unit 1999a). In the USA, for example, declining teenage birth rates (particularly in low income settings) have been thought to be due to the use of long-lasting contraceptives such as implants and injectable methods (Lindsay *et al.* 1999; Social Exclusion Unit 1999a).

Where regular contraception has not been used, or has failed, emergency hormonal contraception (EHC) can be used up to 72 hours after unprotected sex. Since the publication of the UK government's teenage pregnancy strategy, there has been an emphasis on extending young people's access to EHC, for example through school-based nurses, local pharmacies and general practices. There is evidence to suggest that more young people are accessing emergency contraception through these routes (Krishnamoorthy *et al.* 2008).

Young people now, more than ever before, have available to them a wide range of safe contraceptive methods which can not only prevent pregnancy but also help limit sexually transmitted infections. Furthermore, access to contraceptive services for young people has been further facilitated by a range of national guidance on developing good quality services that are easy to reach, have friendly staff, ensure confidentiality and are tailored to the needs of young men as well as young women (Royal College of General Practitioners and Brook 2001; Teenage Pregnancy Unit 2000, 2001).

YOUNG PEOPLE'S ATTITUDES TO ABORTION

Across Europe, England is reported to have one of the highest rates of abortion among women under 20 years of age (European Commission 2000). In 2006, for example, 49 per cent of conceptions to women under 18 ended in abortion – rising to 60 per cent in those under 16 years old (DCSF, 2008). However, rates of abortion across England are not uniform, and significant regional variations exist, with fewer young women having abortions in the least affluent areas (Social Exclusion Unit 1999a).

Earlier research has shown that there is often a degree of aversion towards adoption (particularly among those from lower socio-economic groups) as well as antipathy towards abortion (particularly among younger women) (Allen and Bourke Dowling 1998; Burghes and Brown 1995; Kalmuss, Brickner and Cushman 1991; Social Exclusion Unit 1999a). More recently, Lee *et al.* (2004), in their study of the associations between demographic and socio-economic variables and frequency of abortions among pregnant young women aged 17 years and under, concluded that social deprivation was the primary factor in explaining variability in abortion rates nationally. Importantly, however, after accounting for deprivation and the availability of abortion services, the study also concluded that the proportion of pregnancies ending in termination for all women, including those under 18 years, was similar within the same geographic areas. This indicated that familial or community cultures and norms appear to impact on decision making in relation to abortion. Turner's (2004) study among young women in Scotland concluded that young women who became pregnant from more economically deprived backgrounds were more likely than other young women to continue with the pregnancy rather than have an abortion and to perceive fewer negative implications of becoming a parent.

Furthermore, pressures not to have an abortion may often come from the prospective father of the baby (Allen and Bourke Dowling 1998). For young women living in more affluent areas, there appears to be a greater social acceptance of abortion. As a result, they may not only experience greater family pressures to have a termination but also have fewer opportunities to talk about their decisions with someone outside the family context (Cragg Ross Dawson Ltd 1999; Smith 1993; Tabberer *et al.* 2000).

BECOMING A PARENT

Despite the shift in focus of government policy towards addressing the more complex and underlying contributors to early pregnancy such as inequalities in health and social exclusion, being under 18 years of age and pregnant is still widely viewed as a social problem. To some extent, this can hold true in general terms for both the young mother and her child. There may, for example, be greater obstetric risks for those women who are very young, as well as risk of low birth weight, and higher risk of infant mortality and maternal depression. There can also be reduced educational opportunities, negative employment outcomes, dependence on benefits and adverse housing outcomes (DH 2007; Social Exclusion Unit 1999a).

Young fathers, too, can be portrayed as problems, unconcerned with the mother of their baby – or even the baby itself (Allen and Bourke Dowling 1998; Pollock 2001). Compared with young men without children, teenage fathers have been reported to be more likely to have engaged in law-breaking and truancy and to have left school at 16 (although there is limited evidence of a direct causal effect between dropping out of education and fatherhood) (Dearden, Hale and Woolley 1995). However, like young mothers to be, potential young fathers can experience shock at discovering a pregnancy, can find the realities of parenthood difficult to manage, may be uncertain from where to obtain help and receive little or no encouragement or support to adjust to their role as fathers (Davis 2001; Quinton, Pollock and Golding 2002; Speak, Cameron and Gilroy 1997; Tyrer *et al.* 2005).

Although becoming a young parent can present difficulties for young people, there is evidence to show that access to appropriate advice and support services can affect the health and well-being outcomes for young mothers and their children. Promoting access to antenatal care, and providing social support and educational opportunities for the mother and child have all been shown to have a positive impact on health and well-being outcomes (Chambers *et al.* 2001; NHS Centre for Reviews and Dissemination 1997).

Indeed, it could be questioned whether it is teenage parenthood, in and of itself, that leads to poor outcomes, or whether there are other factors involved. Findings from some studies, for example, have high-lighted the role of socio-economic deprivation in predisposing young people to poverty – irrespective of whether they have a child (Daguerre and Nativel, 2006; Hanna 2001; Phoenix 1991).

In recent years, there has been an increasing literature that questions the view that becoming a parent at a young age ultimately has negative consequences for young people and children and, rather, suggests that early parenthood may also have positive implications for some young people (see, for example, Arai 2003; Barn and Mantovani 2007; Duncan 2007). Often under-reported are the more positive aspects of becoming a parent – particularly where young people find themselves challenged in contexts of family poverty, homelessness and social deprivation where educational and employment opportunities are limited (Barn and Mantovani 2007; Hanna 2001). For some young people, having children provides them with excitement and pleasure and also, to an extent, a new social identity associated with independence, prestige and some degree of status (Hoffman, Thornton and Manis 1978; Michaels and Brown 1987; Musick 1993; Tabberer *et al.* 2000).

Young mothers and fathers often value their role as parents – and becoming a parent can improve a young person's relationship with their own families (Hanna 2001; Tabberer *et al.* 2000). For those young women experiencing disruption and distress in their lives, becoming a mother can ground them in a relationship with someone they care for and love (Barn and Mantovani 2007; Corlyon and McGuire 1999; Knight, Chase and Aggleton 2006).

THE HEALTH AND WELL-BEING OF LOOKED AFTER YOUNG PEOPLE

As of 31 March 2007, some 60,000 children were looked after in England (which is broadly the same as the previous year's figure of 60,300). Overall, the main reason why social services first engaged with these looked after children was because of abuse or neglect (62 per cent) and this percentage has changed little between 2002 and 2007 (DCSF 2007a).

Although the majority of those looked after were of White British origin (74 per cent), around 7 per cent were unaccompanied asylum-seeking children. More generally, since 2003 the number and percentage of children and young people of White British origin has decreased, from 47,300 (77 per cent) in 2003 to 44,700 (74 per cent) in 2007. As of 31 March 2007, 3300 unaccompanied asylum-seeking children were looked after. (This figure has changed little since 2004; however, it represents an increase of 49 per cent from the 2003 figure of 2200.) A little under one-third were of African origin and around one-fifth were from Asian backgrounds with one-fifth from 'other ethnic groups' (DCSF 2007a). As of 31 March 2007, 71 per cent (42,300) of looked after children were in a foster placement. This is an increase of 2 per cent on the previous year's figure of 41,700 and an increase of 3 per cent from 2003 (41,000).

There were 24,700 children who ceased to be looked after during the year ending 31 March 2007 (a decrease of 5 per cent from the previous year's figure, and the figure for 2003 was broadly the same as the 2007 figure). The percentage of children who ceased to be looked after and who were aged 16 and over increased over the five years from 27 per cent in 2003 to 33 per cent in 2007. The proportion of children of White British ethnic origin who ceased to be looked after decreased from 76 per cent in 2003 to 68 per cent in 2007 whereas the proportions of young people from other Asian backgrounds and of African ethnic origin have increased from 1 per cent in 2003 to 3 per cent in 2007 and from 4 per cent in 2003 to 6 per cent in 2007 respectively (DCSF 2007a).

Although all young people can face times of challenge and transition, this holds true particularly for young people who have been looked after by a local authority.[1] Many looked after children and young people have experience of distressing and damaging events prior to their entry into foster or residential care (Macleod 1997; Shaw 1998) and while they are in care. For example, looked after young people have reported feeling uninvolved in decisions made about their placements and inadequately prepared about why they were placed in care (Macleod 1997; Morris and Wheatley 1994; Shaw 1998). Among callers to ChildLine, for instance, looked after children have been among the most isolated and unhappy – many reporting bullying and abuse in their foster or residential placements (ChildLine 2007; Macleod 1997; Morris and Wheatley 1994).

With respect to their education, looked after children and young people do less well than other children and young people (Jackson, Ajayi and Quigley 2003). In part, this is due to high levels of non-attendance at, and exclusion from, schools. On occasions, young people in care run away, thus disengaging from care as well as education services (Wade *et al.* 1998). There are, however, a number of factors that contribute to achievement at school for young people in care. Although, in general, girls in care appear to attain more at school than boys in care, for both, the following factors are associated with achievement:

- having a longest single placement in foster care rather than in residential units

- being placed within the same local authority as the young person's family

- having well-educated carers who give strong support for school attendance and achievement

---

1   The term 'looked after', introduced by the Children Act 1989, refers to a child or young person being 'accommodated by the local authority' for more than 24 hours, either with the agreement of his or her parent(s), if subject to a Care Order passed by a Court, or at the request of a young person over the age of 16. The term 'looked after' is used interchangeably with 'in care' for young people currently looked after, and with 'leaving care' for young people 16 and over who are provided for under the Children (Leaving Care) Act 2000.

- having access to books
- experiencing few extended periods of absence from school
- being involved in activities outside the school and the care system
- having access to an adult who takes a continuing interest in the young person's education and achievements (Bhabra *et al.* 2002; DH 2001b; Jackson and Martin 1998).

Looked after young people have been shown to be more likely to experience significant disadvantages affecting their health and well-being compared with young people more generally (for an overview see Chase, Simon and Jackson 2006). They are more likely, for example, to experience a range of mental health problems (Arcelus, Bellerby and Vostanis 1999; Buchanan 1999) and conduct disorders (Ward and Skuse 2001). Moreover, high rates of self-harming behaviour have been reported – along with suicide attempts, relationship problems, inappropriate sexual behaviour and involvement in prostitution (Richardson and Joughin 2000; Ward and Skuse 2001).

Leaving care can present its own challenges. More often than not, young people leave local authority care at a younger age than young people who leave their family home (Stein 2002) and can be 60 times more likely to be homeless (NCH 2000). Many care leavers are ill equipped for more independent living, with the type of preparation offered not always meeting their needs. Furthermore, the choice of accommodation is limited, as is the support provided during and after the transition to new accommodation (Centrepoint 2006). Problems in finding, moving to and staying in accommodation after leaving care highlight the challenges these young people face: educational disadvantage for too many, leading to experiences of unemployment (or low paid unskilled employment), dependency on benefits and a lack of (or poor) after-care services (Broad 2005; Social Exclusion Unit 1999b; Social Services Inspectorate 2001; Stein 2002).

SEX, PREGNANCY AND PARENTHOOD AMONG YOUNG PEOPLE FROM CARE

Although limited in number, studies of sex, pregnancy and parenthood suggest that young people in and leaving care are more likely to have children in their teenage years than young people who have not been in care (Biehal *et al.* 1995; Brodie, Berridge and Beckett 1997; Corlyon and McGuire 1997, 1999). To date, there has been limited research or evaluation evidence on the types of programme or intervention likely to be most effective in preventing pregnancy among looked after young people (Swann *et al.* 2003) although such programmes have increasingly become a central focus of national policy on reducing teenage pregnancy (DfES, 2006a). The systematic collection of data on pregnancy among young people in public care is a relatively recent development. During the year ending 31 March 2006, there were 400 mothers aged 19 years who were looked after on 1 April 2003, then aged 16 years. However, this figure does not take into account young mothers who have recently ceased to be looked after (DCSF 2007a).

The fact that young people in care receive little or no education about relationships and sex has been cited as one of the reasons for them becoming pregnant in their teenage years. Although this may be an experience shared by young people in general, those in care appear less likely than those who live with their families to have been informed about contraception, pregnancy, physical changes related to puberty, pressures to have sex and sexual feelings (Corlyon and McGuire 1999). There is some evidence to suggest that some young people in care, and particularly in residential care, are more likely to become sexually active at a younger age than young people living with their families. Reasons for this are said to be related to peer pressure to have sex, loneliness and, for those who have been repeatedly let down and rejected, an association between sex and the receipt and giving of affection (Corlyon and McGuire 1997, 1999).

Once pregnant, young women in care may have limited access to counselling, information and advice – each of which could help them to make decisions about what course of action they might best take. Indeed, and even though many young people would not themselves seek an abortion, young women in care have faced considerable pressure to terminate their pregnancy (Barn and Mantovani 2007; Corlyon and McGuire 1997, 1999).

Once they become parents, looked after teenage mothers can encounter considerable difficulties. These include: insufficient education on parenting; limited support from partners and birth families; a sense of social services intrusion into, and regulation and scrutiny of, their lives; and limited availability of after-care support services. All of these can contribute to limited uptake of antenatal and parent craft classes and a mistrust of support provided by Family Centres (Corlyon and McGuire 1997, 1999; Social Exclusion Unit 1999a). In the absence of appropriate support – and also experiencing the problems related to lack of accom- modation, education, employment and money faced by many young people – young parents in and leaving care have been shown to some- times struggle with parenting. Indeed, there is some evidence to suggest that the likelihood of a child of a care leaver being taken into care is higher than that for children who have not been in care (National Foster Care Association 1997), although – as will be discussed in Chapter 8 – there is at the time of writing no systematic data collection to confirm or dispute this claim.

IMPROVING SUPPORT FOR YOUNG PEOPLE IN AND LEAVING CARE

Since the late 1990s, a number of publications and government initiatives have expressed concern about, and proposed actions to improve, the safety and well-being of children and young people in and leaving care more specifically. They include *The Quality Protects Programme* (DH 1998), *Promoting Health for Looked After Children* (DH 1999), *Guidance on the Edu- cation of Children and Young People in Public Care* (DH 2000), the Care Stan- dards Act 2000, the Children (Leaving Care) Act 2000, *Promoting the Health of Looked After Children* (DH 2002), the report on *A Better Education of Children in Care* (Social Exclusion Unit 2003), *The National Service Framework for Children, Young People and Maternity Services* (DH 2004) and the duty in the Children Act 2004 for local authorities to promote the education of children in care.

The outcomes of the 60,000 children in care are reported to be improving. For example, the proportion gaining five General Certificate of Secondary Education (GCSE) passes at grade A*–C has risen from 7 per cent in 2000 to 11 per cent in 2005. The proportion of children in care known to be participating in education, employment or training at age 19 has increased by 8 per cent since 2002 (DfES 2006a). In addition, more care leavers remain in touch with their local authority (from 75 per cent to 89 per cent between 2002 and 2005) (DfES, 2006b).

Compared with earlier legislation, the Children (Leaving Care) Act 2000, which came into effect in October 2001, provided a stronger legal framework for care leavers and appears to have contributed to some of these improved outcomes. Moreover, '[t]here is also evidence of a strengthening of leaving care responsibilities, improved needs assessment, planning and the delivery of financial support, as well as improved levels of support by leaving care teams' (Stein 2005, p.26).

Notwithstanding these improvements, children and young people in and leaving care continue to be at a relative disadvantage compared with children and young people more generally. This holds true, for example, with regard to education (the gap between children in care and children in general gaining five A*–C grades has widened) and mental health (45 per cent of children in care are assessed as having a mental health disorder compared with around 10 per cent of young people generally) (Meltzer *et al.* 2003). Furthermore, certain groups of children, such as those from some minority ethnic communities, are over-represented in the care population.

Most recently, and of particular relevance to the issues discussed here, *Care Matters: Transforming the Lives of Children and Young People in Care* (DfES 2006b) and *Care Matters: Time for Change* (DfES 2007) set out the steps that the government and local delivery partners are to take to improve the outcomes of children and young people in care. In summary, these measures include: improving the role of the corporate parent, providing better support for families and for parenting, making care placements better (and more stable), providing and delivering a first class education, promoting health and well-being (including better provision of education about relationships and sex), improving support for transitions from care placements, and extending the expertise and capacity of practitioners working with children and young people in and leaving care. Further resources are to be provided to realise these ambitions – as well as new models of partnership, including private sector partners (DfES 2007).

It is too early to say what impact these new commitments will have – although we should, perhaps, remain open to their effects being mixed. Experience of a range of policy and programme initiatives since the late 1990s highlights that while some progress can be made, as much remains to be done.

We can, though, remain certain of one thing: that the voices and experiences of young people in and leaving care should lie at the heart of improving provision. As a report of children's views on the UK government's Green Paper *Care Matters* demonstrates (Ofsted 2007a), children and young people are able to provide a clear and concise summary of what should happen next (with many of the points they make echoing the range of issues highlighted in this chapter).

The top ten promises that children want their councils to make to them are (in order, with the most important first): a good home, more of the sort of help already given, more money for specific things like leaving care, to listen to children and act on what they say, better help with education, to keep children safe, more activities, to know that everyone's needs are different, to keep promises made to any child, and to provide a social worker who is effective. Children said that councils need to make and keep pledges to individuals as well as to children generally (Ofsted 2007a).

Children in and leaving care are keen, not only to be listened to, but also to be involved in decisions that affect their lives in care – such as knowing about, being involved in the development of, putting in place and commenting on the National Minimum Standards for children's social care (Ofsted 2007b). Challenges remain in ensuring that they are informed and supported, not only in general matters, but also in those that are specific to being safe and healthy with regard to relationships, sex, contraception, pregnancy and parenthood.

A number of the many legislative and policy developments outlined here in relation to looked after young people and teenage pregnancy are either postscripts to our own study which was conducted between 2001 and 2003, or – like the Children (Leaving Care) Act 2000 – were in their early stages of implementation. Importantly though, and as will be seen in subsequent chapters, all these efforts attune with the range of issues highlighted by young people throughout our research.

In the following chapters, we set our own research findings against this political and policy backdrop and present the experiences of the young people who participated in our study. We provide insights into their lives prior to and during care, into how they learned about sex and relationships and into their experiences of pregnancy, birth and parenthood. In doing so, we aim to situate the events surrounding their becoming mothers and fathers within the wider trajectories of their lives and examine the factors that have helped or hindered them in making decisions about early parenthood and in being able to successfully parent their children. In the final chapter, we revisit some of the legislative and policy underpinnings of government strategies outlined here and reflect on the extent to which they are fit for purpose to fully engage with the often complex lives and circumstances of young people who have not always had the best start in life.

OUR STUDY

The findings presented throughout this book emanated from a DH supported study of *Pregnancy and Parenthood Among Young People In and Leaving Local Authority Care: Determinants and Support for the Mother, Father and Child.* The study was conducted between May 2001 and July 2003 within the Thomas Coram Research Unit at the Institute of Education, University of London. The overall aims of the research were to explore factors contributing to early pregnancy and parenthood among young people in and leaving local authority care; determine the kinds of support available to young parents; and identify what enables or prevents them from receiving the support they need. Overall, the research aimed to inform the development of two key areas of national policy that have grown in importance in recent years, namely teenage pregnancy, and promoting the health and well-being of children and young people looked after.

The work comprised three main elements: first, a review of the relevant international and national literature; second, a national survey of local authorities in England; and, third, a close-focus investigation of the views of young people (either parents or about to become parents) and professionals and carers in four contrasting English sites. This book draws primarily on the findings from the third element of the study – the close-focus, qualitative research with young parents, prospective young parents and professionals and carers providing support. We do, however, also highlight some of the key findings from the survey of local authorities in England (the second element) as and when appropriate. The review of relevant national and international literature (the first element) informed and contextualised both the research itself and this book.

The qualitative research was conducted in four contrasting sites across England – one in the north of England, one in the centre, one in London and one in the south.[2] Sites were selected for geographical diversity, differences in reported rates of teenage pregnancy and variations in approaches to the promotion of sexual and reproductive health among looked young people. Within each site, agreement for the research to take place was obtained from senior managers, and the study took place with the agreement of the local director of social services.

Professionals and carers were selected to participate in the study on the basis of their involvement with, and knowledge of, working with young people in and leaving care, and/or supporting young people in and leaving care, including those who were pregnant and parents. While key strategic and policy-led professionals, such as senior managers in social services for looked after young people and teenage pregnancy coordinators, were interviewed in each of the sites, remaining interviewees were selected in accordance with the nature of service provision within a given area. An average of 20 professionals and carers were interviewed in each site through face-to-face interviews, using a semi-structured interview guide.

Young parents and young pregnant women participating in the study were identified through both statutory and voluntary services. In each of the four sites, an information flyer and a two-page research brief were circulated widely within looked after teams, foster care teams and leaving care teams. To ensure the confidentiality and privacy of young people involved, once potential research participants were identified, a key worker was requested to approach them and ask if they would like to take part in the research. In addition, a wide range of other services poten-

---

2   Approval for the study was sought and received from the Association of Directors of Social Services prior to the selection of the research sites.

tially working with young people in or leaving care was approached. These included Sure Start Plus programmes, local Connexions services, specialist teenage midwifery services, young parents' support groups, voluntary sector organisations, youth offending teams and probation teams, supported housing projects and youth service initiatives including detached youth projects.

The format for interviews with young people was guided by a discussion tool focusing on a number of key areas. These included: their own and significant others' reaction to the pregnancy and subsequent decision making; views about and use of contraception; where young people had learned about issues relating to sexual health and relationships including knowledge of services; who or what had or had not helped them from when they had become pregnant up until the present time; and young people's care history including the age at which they had entered care, and the number and type of placements they had experienced.

The outline discussion guide was pre-tested with a small group of young parents who had been looked after by a local authority not included in the in-depth research. The pre-test provided invaluable guidance to the research team in terms of how, and the order in which, key question areas could best be presented.

Research participants

In total, 63 young people were interviewed: 47 young women between the ages of 15 and 22, and 16 young fathers between the ages of 15 and 23. Although seven young women were older than 20 at the time of the research, all had become parents for the first time at a young age (two at the age of 14, one aged 15, one aged 16, two aged 17 and one aged 18 respectively). All but one of these young women had had more than one child. Both of the young women who had children at age 14, had had three and four children respectively by the time the study was conducted. Likewise, young fathers interviewed in their early 20s had all become parents in their teenage years, and a number were the fathers of several children. Two had become parents at age 16 and had four and three children respectively. Tables 1.1 and 1.2 provide an overview of ages for

Table 1.1 Age of young women at interview and at first becoming parents

Age at interview	14	15	16	17	18	19	20	21	22	Total
Number	–	1	7	10	9	4	9	3	4	47

Age at first becoming a parent	14	15	16	17	18	19	20	21	22	Total
Number	2	5	10	19	9	1	1	–	–	47

Table 1.2 Age of young men at interview and at first becoming parents

Age at interview	14	15	16	17	18	19	20	21	22	23	24	Total
Number	–	1	0	1	3	3	4	–	2	1	1	16

Age at first becoming a parent	14	15	16	17	18	19	20	21	22	23	24	Total
Number	1	1	3	4	2	5	–	–	–	–	–	16

the young women and young men at the time of interview and at the time they became parents.

At the time of the research, there was no obligation on local authorities to collect data on the number of young people within local authority care who had become pregnant or young parents. The survey that was conducted as part of this study with a random sample of local authorities in England indicated that less than 40 per cent of the participating authorities (N=34) could provide any statistical information on the numbers of young women in their care who were either pregnant or had become parents. Even fewer of the participating local authorities (about 25 per cent) were able to provide any data on the numbers of young men in their care who had become fathers.

Given this lack of comparative data at the time of the study, it is not possible to comment on the extent to which the sample of young parents in our study is representative of young parents in and leaving care. This said, there are several reasons that indicate that the findings from our qualitative study are likely to be representative of the experiences of young parents who have lived in public care more generally. First, although the sample of young people was drawn from four very different local authorities, very similar themes emerged irrespective of where young parents were geographically located. Second, the key themes emerging from the study across the four research sites also correlated with those that emerged from the pre-testing of the research tools with a group of young parents from a fifth local authority. Third, the selection of the study sites allowed us to examine young people's experiences of parenthood within local authorities where support services for looked after young people and young parents had varied levels of human and financial resources available and were designed and provided in very different ways. As such, the study was able to capture some of the breadth of the likely experiences of young parents with a varied access to information, advice and support services.

At the time when they were interviewed, 38 of the young women were already parents and nine were pregnant with their first child. Of the young men 13 were already fathers and three were about to become fathers.

In terms of ethnicity, 36 of the young women and 13 of the young fathers were White British, four young women and one young man were of mixed parentage, five young women and one young man described their origins as African, and two young women and one young man were Black British of African-Caribbean heritage. Three of the young women and one young man had been born in Africa and moved to the UK as children.

In total, 78 professionals and carers were interviewed across the four research sites. All were involved in providing support to young people and/or young parents in and leaving care. At each site, participants were selected using a snowballing approach. Initially selected informants were invited to identify other individuals or agencies they felt might have particular knowledge and experience to contribute to the research. Research participants included senior managers of children looked after and leaving care services; teenage pregnancy coordinators; managers of residential care units and residential social workers; foster carers and foster care managers; senior practitioners and field social workers in child and adolescent teams; leaving care social workers and personal advisers (in both statutory and voluntary sector services); specialist nurses for looked after young people; Sure Start Plus advisers; specialist midwives working with teenage parents; family support workers; representatives from youth services and youth offending teams; educational support workers; workers within supported housing units; and representatives from voluntary sector services providing support to young people.

CHAPTER 2

PUTTING PREGNANCY AND PARENTHOOD IN CONTEXT

I just love it. I love my daughter. I've always been one for children. There is no downside, it's brilliant. She changed my life for the better...

INTRODUCTION

Most studies of early pregnancy and parenthood have tended, to date, to inquire into the likely causes of unplanned pregnancies. Some studies, for example, have focused on young people's knowledge of, access to, and use of contraception. Others have questioned the relevance, appropriateness and timeliness of sex and relationships education. Yet, others have highlighted the influences of peer and gender norms, young people's socio-economic and cultural backgrounds, their disengagement from education or their alcohol and drug consumption. A few studies have also examined factors – including those related to gender, class, educational background, age, culture and ethnicity – that can affect the decisions young people make when faced with a pregnancy, such as whether to continue with it or to have a termination.

Notwithstanding the significance of such issues, it is important to recognise how experiences prior to being in care, while in care and in transition from care are reported by young people to have an impact on their lives – not only with regard to becoming pregnant, but also with regard to the decisions made about that pregnancy.

Although our focus was especially on pregnancy and parenthood, we have been struck by the frequency with which a range of issues affected the lives of young people with whom we spoke. These issues included drug use, domestic violence, post-natal depression, homelessness, complex and disrupted family relationships and other challenges such as disabilities. While early pregnancy may be associated with later disadvantage, young people spoke of a number of ways that existing disadvantages in their lives appeared to be ameliorated by becoming a parent. For some young people, at least, early parenthood may well help provide some degree of protection against the challenging circumstances in which they find themselves.

In this chapter, we illuminate some of these issues through four focused case studies which draw on the experiences of five young people – Rebecca, Amanda, Lisa and Dave, and Naomi. We aim to show how, taken together, their experiences of care as well as other significant events shaped their experiences of pregnancy and parenthood. The themes that these young people raised are then explored, in greater detail, through the voices of other young people, in later chapters in the book.

REBECCA

Rebecca, aged 20 at the time of our study, entered care at the age of 12 after her relationship with her mother broke down. Excluded from school at the age of 13, Rebecca was not offered any alternative educational provision. She experienced both foster and residential care; it was while she was in residential care at the age of 12 that she became aware of the lives of other, older, young people around her, who introduced her not only to clubbing but also to sex.

> When I was in care at around 12 everybody was having sex so I wanted to try it. The older ones in the home took me out clubbing at 12 and outside the home they were having sex. I was really drunk the first time, I used no contraception, and didn't even start my periods 'til I was 14.

Despite being sexually active from the age of 12, Rebecca felt that she was not really prepared for this. Her mother had put Rebecca on the Pill at the age of 12 when she suspected from talking to Rebecca's sisters that

Rebecca was having sex. Rebecca stated that she did not realise that the 'tablet I'd been taking since I was 12 was a contraceptive, until I was 15'. Sporadic attendance at school meant that Rebecca missed out on any school-based education about sex and relationships and she described feeling too mistrustful of social workers to listen to anything that they told her about relationships and sex.

Aged 17, Rebecca became a parent for the first time. By 20 she had two children aged 3 years and 1 year. Both children were born with a genetic physical disability and, as a result, Rebecca's time was taken up with providing for their particular and intensive care needs.

When Rebecca first became pregnant after just leaving care, she described being very excited – despite the reservations of her partner, who was 22 at the time. She said: 'I was excited, I felt great in myself as I felt I'd done something for myself instead of for other people. He [partner] wasn't too happy, he didn't want me to keep her [the baby]'. Around this time the relationship between Rebecca and her partner ended.

The negative reaction from Rebecca's partner was reinforced by his family, who felt strongly that Rebecca should not continue with the pregnancy:

> None of his family wanted us to keep her and then we split up when I was seven months pregnant. They thought that we were too young and that I would ruin his life. They said that it wasn't his child and that I'd slept with someone else – they wanted him to have tests done. They sat in the local pub working out when we had sex and stuff like that.

Despite the reactions of others, Rebecca did not even consider an alternative to having her baby since it was something that she really wanted. 'I knew I would keep her and no one would change my mind. I had my own flat. I did not consider abortion as it was my baby. I wasn't bothered by my partner's reactions.'

Two years after the birth of her first child, Rebecca's second child was born. Rebecca, though, was unable to spend much time with the new baby since her first child was in intensive care. This made bonding with her new baby particularly difficult.

While she struggled to meet the needs of her children, Rebecca found services that should have met her needs to be frustrating and insensitive.

Her general practitioner (GP) and the midwives she had come into contact with, she felt, had failed to provide her with adequate support: 'I don't trust the GP and midwives don't listen. I was feeling very depressed with the second child and asked for help but was told "It's you", and I felt very low'.

Special equipment, ordered through her health visitor and which she needed for the children, arrived only after irritatingly lengthy delays. Support from antenatal classes she felt she should have received was said to fall short of really providing the knowledge and skills required for parenthood. Rebecca commented:

> They prepare you for delivery but not for the practical things about being a mum, things that you need to know to look after a child. They need someone to show them what to do like sterilising bottles, how to change nappies. They need someone there for them. There should be more support for those who don't have partners or parents around themselves. I think young people need someone to just sit and talk to, it really does help.

Rebecca went on to talk about how, when she was about 16 years old, her relationship with her own mother had begun to improve. Becoming a mother had, she felt, brought an additional benefit of bringing the two of them closer together. Her own mother became a source of very practical support: 'My mum told me the ins and outs of parenthood, she helped train me and help me practise making bottles. She also prepared me for the hard work'.

As well as her mother, a further source of support was her leaving care worker – 'someone', Rebecca said, 'I could talk to'. Moreover, the community nurses from the local hospital had provided ongoing support regarding her children's condition – although she did indicate that occasional respite support would have been immensely helpful to give her a break and a chance to rest.

Rebecca's partner had also proved helpful from the time when her first child was diagnosed with the disability, at the age of about four weeks. At that point he came back into the relationship and had been supportive since that time.

Looking to the future, Rebecca saw herself as primarily caring for her children until they were in full-time education. She had attempted at one time to go back into education herself, through a college computing course, but this coincided with her first pregnancy and as a result she gave up the course. 'When the kids are in full-time education that's when my life will start and I'll do some study again.'

Given that both her children had inherited a complex genetic condition, Rebecca had also made another very important decision about the future: not to have any further children.

> I'm on the Pill now but I'm just waiting for the letter to come through and I'm having my tubes tied. Although I'm young they say I've got high circumstance of having it done as I have only a one in four chance of having a normal baby. People are worried about me having this operation saying that if I split up with my partner that I may want to have more children. But I've got my children.

Regardless of her early difficulties and the other ongoing strains of bringing up two children with specialised needs, Rebecca's enthusiasm for motherhood was striking.

> I love being a mum, I wouldn't change a thing, they are my pride and joy. I love getting woke up by them in the morning and seeing the smile on their faces, getting to look after them…everything is good about being a mum.

AMANDA

Amanda was 16 years old when she first became pregnant. By the age of 18, when we spoke to her, she had a one-year-old daughter. Prior to becoming pregnant, Amanda had been using the contraceptive pill. She had left home, though, not managed to register with a new GP and had run out of contraceptives. Pregnancy was something that she and her partner had already discussed. Although they had not specifically planned the pregnancy, they were both delighted with it: 'I was chuffed, was in heaven, it was brilliant, she's the best thing that ever happened…definitely. He [boyfriend] was chuffed as well, it was the best thing for us you know, us having a baby'.

Amanda was four years old when she entered care for the first time. Although she returned home about two years later, by nine years of age she was moved back into care and experienced a series of care placements as well as returning periodically to her family home. She hated being placed in foster care and often ran away.

> When I was younger I used to go on the run. I needed someone [to help] at that point but there wasn't anyone... I ran away from foster parents and lived on the street. When I look back now and look at what I've made of myself. I have been able to look after myself since the age of about nine.

Amanda spoke about how she would go down to the bus station and eat with homeless people. She would occasionally receive leftover food from local restaurants.

> At one point I slept under loads of sheets around this pole thing. I was with my brother but he got arrested. I ran off and ended up sleeping in the stairs of a block of flats. I don't remember how old I was but about 10 or 11. I was young... I knew if I went back I would get caught...so I thought I would stay on the streets and see my mum during the day.

Amanda lived on the streets on and off for a year or so. During her time in care she experienced somewhere between 10 and 20 different placements, from which she kept running away. 'I just didn't want to stay in social services' [care]', she commented. At one time, she remembers being caught by the police on a major A road and being sent back to a foster placement. There, she met two other young people who introduced her to gas, which she started to take with them.

> I'm glad I stopped when I did 'cos I wouldn't be here now...it freezes your insides up doesn't it? I have been in some really bad states you know what I mean and the best thing that has happened to me is my baby. Nothing will ever happen like that to her... I will always be there for her...it's a good thing that I've been through what I have ...you know what I mean...'cos she's going to have the best in life definitely...she's never going to go through what I've been through...it hurts to even think about it.

Although Amanda was very happy about the pregnancy and about being a mother, she talked about how neither her parents nor any of the numerous foster carers she had stayed with had ever talked to her about sex or relationships or prepared her in any way for growing up. At some length, she reflected on the lack of opportunities to talk and what she saw as some of the consequences of this.

> I think they should at least be someone there if you need to talk to them about sex and things... I could have been one of the ones that didn't want a baby and then you're stuck with a baby. I was one of the lucky ones that

always wanted a child. People out there don't know nothing, there's diseases going around, there's AIDS and most people don't know about it now 'cos someone won't sit them down and talk about it. Like even...I know I shouldn't really talk about this but even when I started my period...I couldn't talk to anyone...believe it or not when I started my period I was in a foster placement and I was scared...I woke up and there was blood on the sheets...and I know it sounds disgusting and stupid but 'cos I didn't know what to do I grabbed the sheet and threw it out the top window and it landed in the garden...she [foster carer] was wondering where my sheets were going...but I didn't know what to do. I was stuck...I didn't know what was happening to me. At that point I didn't know to go in the shop and buy a packet of pads. I didn't know what's what. Eventually I got around it, I sat down and talked to my dad's partner. She wasn't very helpful but at least she got me a packet of pads. I needed someone to sit down and talk to me about life but I had to work it all out for myself.

Amanda had left school at 16, before the end of the school year. But, even while there, she said she missed sex education and said that most of her information about sex came from friends 'going on about it'. Yet their reports of sex were very different from her own experiences:

Most of my friends, they slept with, like, most of the school...but I never slept with any of them...the first person I ever slept with was my current boyfriend, and then I had a baby with him. But I wasn't interested before. I call myself a bit of a tomboy, do you know what I mean? I wasn't interested in boys really, but then I found Mr Right.

Amanda's pregnancy received a very positive response, not only from her boyfriend, but also from his family. Support came, too, from a family support worker (based within social services) who had worked with Amanda over a number of years and to whom she felt close.

Still, being a mother and trying to establish a home with her boyfriend in which to bring up the baby was far from straightforward. Amanda described how she was placed first in inadequate accommodation, then in a holiday park for a week and a half before finally being provided with a flat. This, she hoped, would be where she would settle but, with it being 'infested with fleas', she was then put into bed and breakfast accommodation over a pub. There followed a series of moves:

> then they took us up to another place for a week and a half, then to another, then another, honestly I can't remember, so many places. You should have seen me when I finally got a place. I just sat there and relaxed…my daughter's happy to have her cot back… She'd been sleeping in her buggy for two months.

The multiple moves that Amanda experienced during the pregnancy and after meant that accessing primary care services was also problematic. Her health records went missing, she had not been able to get the support of a health visitor because 'for the last few months I've been here there and everywhere', attended no antenatal classes ('they got cancelled') and at the time of the birth received no consistent antenatal support:

> I've seen about three or four different midwives… I didn't really know them, the midwife who was supposed to be with me wasn't…but I had her quite late [at night]. Afterwards, a special midwife who works with young mums under 18 came to see me for a few minutes but then not again, because I moved again.

Amanda spoke positively of the support that she received from her leaving care worker – one of the few people who had been a constant in her life during the numerous moves she had experienced.

> I'm the sort of person that would prefer to see one person than to see the whole social services department. I don't like people interfering…like if there were like ten social workers that wanted to see me, I would just want to see the one, do you know what I mean? I think that is why my leaving care worker stuck with me so long. I've always hated social services until I met my leaving care worker. I understood a bit more then but…'cos to me all they wanted to do was to take me away.

On a practical basis, the leaving care worker had helped Amanda with equipment for the baby since she herself struggled to do this on the £42 a week provided by social services. Generally, though, her experiences of support from the social services department over the years had been mixed:

> They could be a bit more helpful…they let you down too much as well …they say they are going to be there at a certain time and you get all ready and they don't turn up. Sometimes I have been in situations where I have been stuck…and there's been no one.

Amanda talked about her interaction with other health services since having her baby. She felt that she was 'being watched' and had a great fear of leaving the child, even with the midwives in the hospital, so that she could have a rest. She also talked briefly about the child protection assessment that was carried out and how she felt annoyed that there was an assumption that, because she had been in care, the baby 'would need to be under social services'. 'I hated it [the assessment] but was pleased when it was done. The report was really good, the case was closed, I was not needed to be seen again…I was a certified good mum.'

Although she had not enjoyed school, Amanda regretted, somewhat, leaving it. She said she had plans to go to college later that year to study for a national vocational qualification (NVQ) in health and social care, with a view to becoming a nurse (as she had enjoyed some work as a non-qualified nurse). She planned to study part-time, with her partner working part-time, so that they could share the baby's childcare. Indeed, her partner had been an important source of support throughout the years. 'If I hadn't had him', Amanda commented, 'I don't think I would have been able to cope very well'.

At some point in the future she thought that they would have more children. For the moment, though, she just wanted to enjoy her baby and 'watch her grow up'. As she said about being a mum:

> I just love it. I love my daughter. I've always been one for children. There is no downside, it's brilliant. She's changed my life for the better… I've always been one for caring… I've been told that I care too much…but now I've got someone that I can look after and I've always wanted that.

LISA AND DAVE

Lisa, 22 years old at the time of the study, had entered foster care at the age of 9. After a number of foster care placements which broke down, at the age of 14 she was placed in residential care. Lisa felt that a combination of learning and behavioural difficulties had contributed to the placement breakdowns and the consequent lack of continuity of care and support that she had received. The multiple placement moves resulted in sporadic and disrupted attendance at school which in turn, she said, accentuated her learning and behavioural problems.

Dave, aged 19 at the time of the study, had been placed in residential care when he was 13 years old. Despite being permanently excluded from school at the age of 11, he had been provided with no home tutoring or alternative education. For him, residential care provided particular opportunities to have a series of sexual relationships. 'Care homes are the worst places for early sexual activity: I was sleeping with so many girls when I was there as I think girls are attracted to boys who are on a rough path.'

For Lisa, too, residential care was a time of excessive freedom and very limited support or guidance. She was, she said, introduced early to drugs and to sexual encounters, which she viewed as exploitative. Despite knowing about her relationship with an older man, care staff in the residential home appeared to ignore it – even though her partner would pick her up from the care home and she would stay away for a number of nights. When she did return to the residential unit, she commented: 'They never asked me if I was all right.' In retrospect, Lisa felt that, given her age, more should have been done to question her relationship with her partner.

> I had sex at 14 because it was freedom to me. I was not allowed out when I lived at home while other kids were playing out, so when I got to residential care I felt I could do what I wanted. The man I had sex with was 25. He used to go around the children's homes and seek out girls to have sex with…he was just after sex. He lived with his parents but they were away a lot so I used to go there a lot and that's why I missed so much school. I learned a lot about drugs and other behaviours when I went into residential care.

Lisa and Dave were partners at the time of the study. They had three children together and Dave had fathered one other child. When Dave discovered he was a father for the first time (prior to his relationship with Lisa) he was in 'jail' (a young offenders' institution) and was 15 years old. The mother of the child was an 'older woman' and he found out about the pregnancy through his stepsister, who had come to visit him. He described how he felt that he was just a child himself at the time and did not tell anyone else about the pregnancy of his girlfriend. By the time he got out of jail, the mother of the baby had found another partner. He explained what he thought:

I saw the baby after I got out and my ex said I could be involved, but she was with a partner of her own age and he was good to her so I didn't think it was fair to get involved as the child had taken the new partner as her dad. As long as I knew the baby was looked after and cared about, that's all I cared about.

Lisa became pregnant (for the first time) when she was 14 years old.

I was 14 when I first fell pregnant. I was living in the children's home at the time. No one spoke to me about pregnancy or periods or anything, then I became pregnant. It was only when I missed three periods that the staff put me in for a pregnancy test and I found out I was three months pregnant. It was really, really frightening… I was really unsure about myself.

However, 24 weeks into the pregnancy she had a miscarriage. 'I lost the baby at 24 weeks and didn't get any counselling afterwards and the staff told me to rest in bed but no one explained what had happened to me.'

On discovering that he was to become a father for the second time at 16 years old, with Lisa as his partner, Dave's response was different from that when he first learned he was to be a father.

I remember more at 16 with Lisa, I was shocked and was in jail again, and she told me on the phone she was pregnant, she was a few months gone when she told me. It felt different this time though as I was committed to her, it felt more comfortable, maybe because she had also had a similar care background to me.

Lisa, too, felt differently about her second pregnancy and felt positive about her relationship with Dave and the prospect of having a child. However, there were other complications in their lives. Their addiction to heroin meant that becoming parents was far from straightforward. Lisa said:

With the second child I felt happy, as I was in a nice relationship, and I knew that I'd be looked after…but Dave was in prison when I was pregnant. When he got home I thought we would be really happy living all together as a family, but then it didn't happen that way and I was really sad.

Lisa described why and how their first child was taken into the care of social services:

With our first child we had to go to an assessment centre, they didn't know I was on drugs but they knew Dave was. I wanted him to be assessed too but they took me in first and he came later and was getting no help with his drug problem and I knew that things were going to get messed up and it did. The baby was taken into care.

Dave added:

> We were in an assessment centre [family and baby unit] at the time and we were both fighting quite a lot and I was supposed to be getting help with drug and alcohol abuse. She went into the centre first with the baby and I was allowed to go for day visits and this lasted for two months. She wanted me there and I wanted to be there too, it wasn't right, I was still not getting support. At this stage they moved me in full-time for a month, they put me in there but I wasn't offered any help, I was on medication and so it was a difficult time. I didn't get a worker to support my drug problem so it was as if they were waiting for me to slip up. It wasn't a fair assessment: they knew I could look after the child but I blew it as I got drunk while I was there. They then ended the assessment and took the baby into care. I think they dug the hole and then pushed me in it as they knew I had a problem but didn't get me the help they promised.

Dave and Lisa's struggle with heroin continued throughout the birth and subsequent removal of two further children. At the time of the research both of them were on a methadone programme and were no longer taking heroin. Dave, perhaps more than Lisa, was hopeful of being reunited with their children and on the whole felt quite positive about the support they were receiving from the social services department leaving care service. He commented:

> We weren't straight with social services straightaway about the problem, as heroin has been the main problem, it is that which has caused the problems and the fighting and we are now on methadone. They have said that in a year or so if we show we have kept off it we could have two of the children back.

For Lisa, her reticence in telling social services about their drug problems was linked to earlier experiences of mistrust with the system.

> I thought I could trust social services before [but] when I told them what my mum and dad were doing they took me back home and told them what I had been saying so I started to run away.

She spoke of how, aged 18, she was placed by the social services department in bed and breakfast accommodation where she was violently raped. Furthermore, the fact that having disclosed their drug problems to the leaving care service had resulted in the children being removed confirmed Lisa's feelings of mistrust with respect to the social services department: 'We didn't tell aftercare that me and Dave were on drugs at first...then we did tell them and I thought it would help us if we did tell them, but it didn't.'

She went on to describe how she felt that social services 'set traps' for her and Dave to fall into, like calling the police when they knew that Dave might react violently. Essentially, she felt very bitter about the lack of support provided by the social services department and felt, too, that they had been let down. By contrast, she did feel positive about the support she was receiving from drug and alcohol services at the time of the interview and described how she felt able to talk to staff at this service.

Lisa made several references to her learning problems and how this affected her interaction with the services that she came into contact with. There were few people whom she trusted and her support network, she said, was limited to Dave, his mother – who had taken her in and given her support when Dave was in prison – and particular professionals who she had found easier to relate to, such as the midwives at the birth of her children and the workers in the drug and alcohol service. She commented:

> Sometimes I find it hard to talk to people when they are trying to explain things to me, it's a problem I've got. I find it hard to take in the words they are telling me and knowing what they mean as I'm dyslexic so I end up talking about something completely different. I look to my partner to explain things to me. I wonder sometimes if it is that I'm not able to express what I need or that people just don't want to listen.

NAOMI

At the time of the study, Naomi was 21 years old. She had two children aged four and two. She lived with the father of her second child and they were planning to be married in the near future. From age eight, Naomi had experienced a series of care placements – both residential and foster care. She preferred residential to foster care as she did not get on with her foster carers' own daughter.

However, Naomi felt that, in residential care, negative rather than positive behaviours were rewarded. She dwelled on the confusion and mixed messages about rules and behaviour within the residential home that she struggled to make sense of:

> When I first went to the home I was going to school every day for ages and going to clubs but then in the home people were smoking dope, not going to school, doing what they wanted. You realise that you don't have to go to school every day and you can stay there and get new trainers like everyone else. People that went out burgling cars were getting new tracksuits. Yet I was going to school and getting nothing.

Although doing well at school, her first boyfriend and the freedom this relationship brought, affected her attitude to, and attendance at, school.

> At 15 most of my friends were having sex before me but I wasn't. I had lots of other interests (army cadets, drama school etc.) and I was doing well at school. It was once I started going with my boyfriend and that I was absconding all the time from the home. I got my last chance to do my GCSEs, 'cos I'd been staying out all the time and staying with him, but I didn't do them. It was suddenly being able to do what you want for a change I think that made me focus on the relationship and it was that first love, you feel like you are doing what 'you' want for a change.

Although not planned, Naomi was 'really happy' when she found out she was pregnant. She did not consider any option other than having her baby:

> I knew there was no other choice for me than to have the baby. I wouldn't consider abortion as I'd got myself pregnant so I'd have to deal with it. I couldn't give a baby away after being pregnant so didn't think about fostering or anything.

Her pleasure at being pregnant and having a baby was, Naomi suggested, linked to her own lack of experiences of being loved.

> With my first child it's like having someone of your own to love as I'd never had that, and especially if you've been on your own a lot like me. I think that's why I was so over the moon when I got pregnant. It's almost like you

have given yourself a purpose, some security… I think that's why people in homes may have them.

Her partner at the time of her first pregnancy was happy about becoming a father and was present at the birth of their daughter. But, soon after that, he seemed to lose interest in his girlfriend and his daughter. Naomi stated that, when she had stayed at her partner's mother's house for a few days following the birth of their daughter, he was never around. She talked, too, of how her feelings about her partner had influenced her decision about having the baby; she believed she was in a relationship that would last. However, her own life and that of her daughter's became increasingly difficult after she moved in with her boyfriend – soon finding out what an aggressive person he could be.

When I moved to the flat he was violent and in the end he held a knife to me and took the baby and the pram off me and I had to go around to his mum and sister and get help. They knew what he was like but I used to cover up for him all the time. She [his mum] called the police and they took me to a refuge, as I didn't want my daughter around that, so I went but I hated it and only stayed for two days and then I ended up getting some digs. I put my name down on the homeless list and got a place straightaway. So I just moved away from him and have only seen his sister once. He was violent when I was pregnant but after I had the baby I started going mad when he started lifting his hands to me… I realised all the stress I went through when I was having the baby and that it wasn't right.

Such violence and stress, Naomi worried, had an effect on her daughter: 'The baby was biting and scratching even when she was one and two and I was thinking was it because of all that stress when she was a baby?'

Currently with another boyfriend, her fiancé, Naomi nonetheless felt anxious when she had become pregnant by him. Even though she was not taking contraception, she said '[I felt] upset with myself that I had let this happen again'. While resolved to continue with this second pregnancy, she described having mixed feelings about how her partner would react to it.

I'd known my partner about a year and we'd been seeing each other three or four months when I got pregnant. I was still shocked but happy. I thought, 'How have I let this happen after just getting over the baby stuff with my first child?' I knew I was pregnant like the first time. I was worried about telling him in case he thought I had done it on purpose, but then I thought, 'I don't care in any case if he doesn't want anything to do with me, I'll get on with it – I'm pregnant now!' I was a bit concerned about having a man in my life again anyway after getting bitten the first time.

Life became difficult again for Naomi as a result of severe post-natal depression after having her second child.

I should have been very happy after the second child. I had a nice home and everything but my health started going downhill, my hair started dropping out. I had it [depression] for about two years, I turned into a different person.

Although she sought help for her depression from her GP, Naomi found him to be quite dismissive of her symptoms:

I didn't get any help with my post-natal depression. I was worried as the kids were ill all day and I couldn't get them seen but when I got in he told me to slow down and not to panic. He told me to go back in two weeks and I went and he said I was all right, but I realised I had post-natal depression. I was living in a new place with two children and I changed, I went from happy-go-lucky to really miserable. I had panic attacks and anxiety and my boyfriend used to say I had depression but the doctor said I was all right. I got *myself* back together really slowly and realised what was happening. I don't think I even looked in the mirror for about two years.

Through both pregnancies, Naomi had a somewhat volatile relationship with her own mother – whose reaction to the first pregnancy had been 'mixed'. Although planning to live with her mother after having the baby, she felt that her mother feared that she would be left to look after the baby. Her first pregnancy coincided with a time when she was just managing to rebuild a relationship with her mother.

I was 16 and I'd just started talking to my mum again after being in homes for two years and she came with me when I found out I was pregnant and I was over the moon, she was dead supportive. I had a care order on me still when I started talking to my mum again. My mum said she wanted the care order taken off us and that was taken off. I was supposed to be living with her but I didn't get on with my brother so I was living in a flat with my boy-friend and it was all mouldy and that and I got bronchitis and then my mum was keeping in touch with me and buying the shopping and things for the baby as she was getting child benefit for me.

Although her relationship with her mother appeared to be going well, it deteriorated to such an extent that Naomi had, once more, to stay away from her mother's home.

She pinched my maternity grant and pinched all the baby stuff. I had planned to move back to my mum's thinking it would be all right even with the problems with my brother because he's really bad with noise. But I wasn't really keen on it but thought I would have to. But when she'd done that, stole my money, I didn't want anything to do with her so got my own private flat the day I was due.

Since that time, however, Naomi's relationship with her mother improved to the extent that her mother now regularly looked after the children. Naomi felt that her mother's opinion of her had changed: 'She sees I have my own kids and that I'm a mum and it's different. She has them every other weekend now'.

By contrast, the mother of Naomi's ex-partner had provided enormous support to her throughout her first pregnancy and immediately after she gave birth:

When the baby was born everything was sorted and bought for me, she went to second-hand shops and got me sorted, she gave me practical advice and helped me get the baby into a routine. She showed me how to sterilise bottles and bathe her properly. She helped me as you are so tired and she helped me.

Naomi recognised that with parenthood came new demands. She was no longer able, for example, to lie in; if she ever went out at night she still had to get up early the next day. The reality and responsibility of parenthood came as a shock to her. 'I knew when I was pregnant the first time it would mean more responsibility but it wasn't until she was born that it hit me like a ton of bricks.'

Being able to go back into education has, among other things, helped Naomi to deal with her depression. At the time of the interview she was doing a hairdressing course and felt that this was helping her to cope. Earlier attempts to return to college to study Maths and English after her first child proved too difficult through lack of childcare. The leaving care service had also provided practical support and she described the leaving care workers as 'people you can talk to'.

Naomi clearly enjoyed having her children and bringing them up. For her, the best part of being a parent was:

> Seeing the children smile, taking them to school and on day trips, everything… They keep you smiling…you haven't got time to sit around and feel sorry for yourself as they keep you busy. They are just a pleasure to have really. I don't know what to do with myself when they are not around. I do want to go out now and then but not like I used to.

For these young people at least, their experiences of being pregnant and being a parent, despite difficulties along the way, were generally positive. Becoming a parent brought new responsibilities, yet also new opportunities: to a secure family life that they themselves had never had; to a sense of stability in their lives; and to opportunities to build secure and strong emotional attachments.

However, the extent to which individuals were able to make the most of these responsibilities appeared often to depend on whether they had, or were provided with, the means to mitigate the more challenging aspects of being a young person and a young parent.

While there were some commonalities in young people's accounts of their lives, such as disrupted family relationships, the lack of quality sex and relationships education or the need for good quality accommodation, there were differences too. Lisa and Dave, for example, highlighted that more could have been done to assist them with their dependency on heroin. Naomi spoke of the assistance she received when she found herself with a violent partner. Rebecca spoke of the specialist support she needed to be the best mother she could to her disabled children.

Yet there were other commonalities, too. Each young person strove to make the best they could of the challenging circumstances in which they found themselves. By giving a voice to young people we can, perhaps, best understand their strengths and needs – building on what they themselves bring to pregnancy and parenthood, and providing assistance where needed. In the chapters which follow, we explore a number of themes voiced here by Rebecca, Amanda, Lisa and Dave, and Naomi, and highlighted further by other young people who took part in the study.

CHAPTER 3

BEING YOUNG, BEING IN CARE

I came out of the residential home when I was six years old and went to my Nan's house – I left my Nan's for beatings and things like that. Ever since 13, I've been out there...staying all over...here, there, friend's house, under stairway of flats... I've done it all.

INTRODUCTION

Children and young people in the UK who, for whatever reason, cannot live with their birth families are mostly looked after in either residential or foster care. When talking with young people in the study, our initial focus was on the type and number of placements they had experienced. However, young people soon alerted us to the importance of finding out more about their experiences of care and their reasons for being looked after. These, they said, had an important impact on their current circumstances.

As young people talked about events that had led to them being in care, it became clear that many had experienced complex and volatile family relationships, domestic violence, having caring responsibilities at a young age, and various forms of abuse. With these, came feelings of rejection and abandonment. Some young people had entered care as babies or young children. Around one-quarter of the young people entered care for the first time between the ages of 12 and 15 years.

Once in care, there were often negative as well as more positive experiences. Some young people had been placed in both residential and foster care and many spoke of multiple placements, often interspersed with periods back at home with their parents.

LIVES BEFORE CARE

Several young people we spoke with – particularly those living in the London site – had been born or lived in other countries before coming to the UK. They often described a series of challenging transitions: moving to England, adapting to a new culture and way of life, and entering the care system, all occurring within a few years or months of each other.

Adejoke, for example, arrived in the UK from Nigeria with her siblings and her mother when she was 10 years old. She described how difficult it was at first:

> It was a different environment; everything was different or shocking. And you have to try and get to know the new people. 'Cause you could get bullied as well, 'cause they don't like the way you look or… I had proper friends when I got to Year 10. Year 7, 8 and 9 and primary school I didn't really make friends.

Ese also moved to the UK from Nigeria, arriving when she was only two years old to live with her grandmother. She described receiving a very strict upbringing combined with feelings of rejection from her own parents, who were still in Nigeria and never contacted her. As a result of the lack of freedom she had and the strain this placed on her relationship with her grandmother, social services became involved and the possibility of her going into foster care was introduced. Ese painted a vivid picture of the culture clash she felt absorbed in – being Nigerian by birth but being brought up in Britain:

> This is the problem. I was never taught how to speak Nigerian. So I find it quite offensive when Nigerian people look down at me because I can't speak my own language. But my Nan never ever taught me how to speak Nigerian.

Despite being in the UK since the age of two and speaking only English, Ese went on to explain how she did not have British citizenship and her legal status in the UK remained uncertain, a situation that was bound to exacerbate her feelings of insecurity and confusion around her identity:

I see myself as Nigerian. I always say I'm Nigerian 'cos I haven't got a British passport. That's another issue. When I left home, that's when I found out that I hadn't got a passport. My Nan has never solved the immigration thing. So I have been doing that myself. And my solicitor has just said that I've got indefinite leave to remain at the moment and I have to apply for it [the passport] next year which I find really out of order 'cos I was brought into this country.

Joseph, aged 20 at the time of the study, was originally born in Sierra Leone and moved to the UK at the age of eight to be reunited with his mother, who had already been in the UK for about two years at that time. His mother had brought himself and his brother to the UK so that they could be together and so that they would have access to a good education. After his mother returned to Sierra Leone when he was about 13 years old, Joseph looked after himself and his younger brother for a couple of years before they were both taken into foster care. Joseph said that he had no regrets that he had been given so many responsibilities at such a young age and had no resentment of the fact that his mother had left them and returned to Sierra Leone.

It has made me a stronger person, because somebody told me there is a reason for everything. So, I didn't feel any resentment. My brother, I think, did. Because he was young, he wasn't really understanding what was going on. He is only a year younger than me, but still he's a bit younger in the mind. I think he felt resentment towards my mother, but I didn't. I knew that there was a reason for her doing what she did. Because if I'm resenting, that's just like a waste of time and energy – I could be doing something better.

Other young people we spoke to had experienced stormy and abusive relationships with parents prior to entering the care system. Some of them attributed these difficulties to their birth parents, while others reflected that they themselves, through their behaviour, had led to the breakdown in relationships with their parents.

Mary described a very strict Catholic upbringing against which she started to rebel when she was about 12. She was not allowed to have any friends and had to give up playing netball, a sport at which she excelled. At this point, she started to be physically abused by her father. She was placed on the child protection register and went into residential care.

Janet, on the other hand, talked of how her mother could not cope with Janet's own 'evil' behaviour, and a number of other young people, particularly young women, described how their own behaviour had pre-cipitated or contributed to their pathway into the looked after system.

Adejoke also experienced a breakdown in her relationship with her mother and as a result went into residential care when she was aged 13. She spoke about the strict rules and restrictions on her freedom that her mother imposed, conditions which, in her view, caused this breakdown. She finally went into care when her mother started physically abusing her:

> I have to be back home ... at the beginning I had no friends anyway, but I had to be back home at 4 o'clock or I would get beat...so I would have to be rushing home 3.30 after school. Like it's not fair. Like other kids are just outside, having fun or going to the shop or going to the park. And I had to rush home to do work like clean up the house.

Some young people experienced difficult relationships with step-parents, often sharply contrasting with the affection they felt towards a birth parent. Ellie was 17 when we spoke to her. She was born in Nigeria to a Nigerian father and Ghanaian mother and moved to England at the age of 13. Ellie described her closeness to her father which she said created serious difficulties between herself and her stepmother. Things became even more complex when her stepmother involved her church:

> She [my stepmother] was jealous of me and my dad because we were close...she would go and complain to my dad. So, me and my dad got into an argument. And we went to this African church and they said I was a witch. Because my step-mum hasn't got a child they say I am the one that is holding her back from having a baby – that I'm cursing everything. I am the one that is bringing problems home and everything.

David, aged 17 at the time of the research, described his and his brother's reactions to witnessing his stepfather being violent towards his mother.

> My mum says love is a mad thing. She took my step-dad back even though he'd hit her. Me and my brother went mad with him. We hung him off a balcony by his ankles in a top floor flat. Now he's a hard geezer, he's been in jail himself. He's a fighter. But we weren't scared 'cos no one hits my mum and gets away with it.

Feelings of being rejected and abandoned by their parents, most notably by their mothers, were frequently expressed by young people. Janet said:

> I was in touch with my mum when I was about 13, 'cos she told me she didn't want to see me and she got reports that I still wasn't behaving and she sent me a card when I was 12 saying she didn't want to see me any more. It didn't help much…it just makes you worse hearing stuff like that.

Similarly, Susie described her abandonment as a baby by her mother and her later rejection by her father and latterly by an aunt, who had thrown her out of her home when she was 15:

> I have no family. All the family have abandoned me. I would never forgive her [my aunt] because she was always going on about my mum…and how my mum always knew what a bastard I would turn out to be and that's why she abandoned me at five weeks.

Tamsin and Anna both had older siblings and felt rejected from birth by their mothers, who they said, did not want any more children. Tamsin explained:

> I wish I could be like my sister. I could be out on the street and my mum would not think of helping me. All my life I have just wanted my mum to like me and accept me for what I am. My mum only planned to have two kids… she didn't want me… I am the black sheep of the family.

For Susie, it was the knowledge that her mother had intended to have her aborted that epitomised her sense of rejection:

> My mum tried doing it [having a termination] with me and if it hadn't been for my dad, I wouldn't have been here 'cos my mum never wanted me, she only wanted one and she had that one and then she got pregnant with me. It doesn't make you feel very good about yourself.

RESIDENTIAL CARE

A small number of young people described their experiences in residential care in positive terms. When they did, they almost always focused on the good relationships they had established with residential care staff. Amy, who was 18 when we spoke with her, having had her son at the age of 15, clearly valued very specific elements of the relationship that she had with care staff:

> There were four members of staff that were lovely, but there was one who was very judgemental… They were kind and loving…and they said it was all right to talk to them whenever I needed it… They were lovely.

Mandy also spoke highly of the staff in her care home, but the relationships that they evidently nurtured were not enough to prevent her from regularly absconding from the residential unit: 'They [residential workers] were really supportive, they were always supportive…. I've always been able to go up to them and tell them, they have always been supportive, support you in whatever decision you make.'

That said, Mandy still returned with her baby to the care home every weekend for lunch and she described how her former link worker still frequently visited her once she had moved to her own home – helping her with tasks such as decorating and shopping.

Similarly, Claire reflected on the fact that, although she had perhaps not appreciated the residential care staff at the time, her former key worker had continued to be a lifeline for her, had recently been to visit – bringing her clothes for the baby – and sent her Christmas and birthday cards every year. She commented:

> And that sort of relationship to still be there after all I have put them through and the names I called them…and for them to still be there for me, it just shows that they are really not as bad as you made them out to be when you were living with them.

Yet most young people who had spent time in residential care were most likely to describe negative experiences there. Many spoke of being introduced to drug taking, truancy and exploitative relationships. Mary described her time in residential care as one of turmoil, violence and unhappiness: 'I was in residential care for three years but kept running away…there were people on drugs and I got beaten up because I wouldn't take part. I learnt about unhealthy relationships through what was going on there.'

Looking back and reflecting upon their experiences in care, some of the young people we spoke with admitted how much they pushed the boundaries set by those looking after them in the care system, often a reaction to their sense of being dumped or uncared for. Claire, for example, said it was easier to reflect on her behaviour retrospectively but that at the time it felt like a logical response to feelings of abandonment and rejection:

> You always play up the staff at a children's home…but it's not until you move out that you realise that they are only there to help… You do anything you can to really annoy them. I kept running away, coming in late…but that's what you do when you are that age…and it makes it so much harder because you are being told that your parents don't love you…it's not social services that are saying that, it's your so-called friends that are trying to make you feel better, but it makes you feel worse, like you are on your own, not wanted.

Brandon was 20 when we spoke with him and had become a dad a year earlier. Placed in a residential care home at the age of 13, he vividly reiterated such feelings of rejection and isolation in residential care: 'In children's homes, there is nothing. It makes you feel like you are unwanted because there are all unwanted children around you…you are unwanted as well.'

FOSTER CARE

The quality and types of foster care placements described by young people were often variable too. Many had experienced a series of placements – both good and bad they told us. Mary, for example, had run away from one foster carer before she met another care professional through friends to whom she could relate more straightforwardly. 'She was just a good person to talk to and I am sure if I had stayed with her as a foster mum, I wouldn't have run away.'

While some young people were negative about being in foster care because they felt unloved and uncared for, others felt positive about the experience because the foster carers had treated them 'like their own' and 'part of the family'. These young people tended to refer to their foster carers as 'mum' and 'dad'. James was 22 and had a four-year-old son at the time of the study. He commented about his foster carers: 'I have a good relationship with them. They are like my mum and dad and I have been with them for 11 years. I get guidance from my mum and dad [the foster carers].'

Georgia, who was aged 21 at the time of the study – and who had the first of her three children when she was 14 – described her foster carers as being her main source of support. A number of other young people also talked of the ongoing relationship that they had maintained with a foster carer after they had left their care. Foster carers often provided ongoing support when young people discovered they were pregnant or after having the baby.

Of the young people who were very negative about their time spent in foster care, many were critical of a social services system which, in their view, had not prepared them adequately for foster care. Some felt that they had been set up to fail. Poppy commented: 'They never made an effort to put me into the right foster placement.'

Emma was adopted at the age of 18 months but unfortunately her adoptive placement broke down when she was 15. She was sexually abused while living with her adoptive family although not by her adoptive parents. Consequently, Emma went into foster care at the age of 15, but had criticisms about how this transition was handled:

> Foster carers were nice but living with them was not too nice. It's like being dumped into a family that you don't know…there weren't no work done with them…like meeting with them first…or covering some of my issues…like I was molested and that…that wasn't mentioned…there was no work between us to build the relationship…that's why it kept breaking down I think. The social worker should have come and worked with us a little…but it wasn't like that.

Karen was similarly critical of what she saw as a lack of preparation for going into foster care. She had experienced several foster placements which kept breaking down partly, she told us, as a result of people not being transparent about the process of moving into care:

> Foster placements usually end at a point where I either just throw something at the foster carer or I just get so abusive she can't deal with it any more…so I think all right you're going to put me into another foster placement where I am more likely to get into that situation…because they put me in placements but they don't sit down and say…this is what the person's name is…you don't get to meet the person before you go…so there isn't any rapport there or anything so you are just ending up with people you don't know…and they suddenly put all these boundaries on

you…and as a child in care you don't respond well to that at all…no good at all. I actually think the care system is set up to make children fail and not succeed and I intend on suing them when I get older.

For some young people, 'care' was far from what they experienced while living with foster families. Bridget had had three foster placements. She remembered getting on well with the first foster carer. However, a subsequent carer was abusive and she was locked in her room even though she had done nothing wrong. Claire went into care on a full care order when she was four, was with one foster carer for three years and then another for seven years. On referring to this second foster family she said: 'I played them up something chronic because their son sexually abused me for two years, so I did everything I could do to get out of there.'

Brandon talked of how he was exposed to hard drug use in foster care and subjected to racist abuse:

The son of the foster mum was a 'junkie' and he used to warm up barrels of heroin showing us how he does it. I am 13 at this stage…get mad over everything and a White person calling me a Black dickhead every day I get up…in a White foster home – one light-skinned foster mother – part from that I am the only Black one. Everyday because he was high all the time with the browns and that – he was always calling me a 'nigger' and accusing me of stealing his things.

Often as a result of strict boundaries or the mistreatment and/or abuse that they had experienced in foster care, some of the young people we spoke to ran away regularly from foster care. Adejoke, for example, did so repeatedly:

I always used to go into foster care but I never stayed there for long. They always used to try and send me back home and I would run away again. Yeah, so I didn't have that close bond with my foster carers.

Similarly, David described reacting against the overly authoritarian approach of his foster carers: 'I always ran away. They [the foster carers] were really strict and over the top. If I was five minutes late they'd take a fiver off me pocket money and things like that.'

And for Mary it was a combination of being placed with carers within whom she did not feel at ease and increasingly restrictive curfews that lead to her frequently running away from her placement.

MULTIPLE PLACEMENTS

Moving in and out of care, between foster placements and between residential and foster care was a common pattern for a number of young people. There were a number of reasons for this, such as young people running away from abuse, maltreatment or what they felt were overly strict environments, or being returned to birth families – sometimes due to there being a lack of social services funding to continue a placement (usually a foster placement), once a young person reached a certain age.

The result of such constant change was that many young people felt a fundamental sense of instability and a mistrust of social care and other systems and services. Karen, for example, had been through 12 different placements. She explained not only how difficult it was to be constantly moving around but also what it felt like having to enter a new placement.

> It's quite distressing actually. Sometimes you get immune to it after a while…like with me, on my own, I've got immune to situations…I just go into the home, mind my own business, you mind yours and we'll get along fine. That's what happens when you keep moving children all over England, 'cos I have lived from Essex to Bucks…to up here, to down there, to everywhere…it doesn't help…how do you move a child that's grown up in south London to Essex and expect them to be normal and behave well there. …they [social services] just live in this fantasy world of children who adapt to certain things. …we're not chameleons. …we don't adapt.

Miranda's experience was typical of many young people we spoke with, moving between placements and then back home to her mother when things were calm enough at home. She explained why living with foster carers can be difficult:

> I was in care from when I was 10, fostered from when I was 12 till now [age 16]…I was in respite for a bit. I always used to fight with my mother – we are too alike and sometimes we didn't get on. Between 10 and 12, I was all over the shop – different foster carers, it's difficult when they have kids of their own. From 15 and a half to 16 and a half I had another two foster placements as I'd had a big fight with my mum. Since I moved out, it's been brilliant. I think that's why I went to live with my [real] mum because the last foster placement I was in they were all right but I couldn't do anything they were so strict – they just treat you like a six-year-old.

FEELINGS ABOUT BEING IN CARE

Feeling stigmatised, discriminated against or prejudged as a result of having a care history angered some young people who resented the stereotyping that they felt accompanied children in the care system. Mary explained: 'There are a lot of stereotypes about kids in care… They think we are all rascals who are on drugs and go around vandalising everything and that's not true.'

As a result of such attitudes, some young people, like Rebecca, described a need to 'forget' their past: 'That's my past and I don't want to go back to my past…it's a fresh start for me from now on.'

Other young people put forward their own ideas about how the experience of care more generally could be improved or even prevented in the first place. Amy, based on her own personal experiences, held strong views on this issue:

> I think the worst thing is family separation…rather than splitting up families – my little sisters live in Birmingham and I only get to see them for six hours a year. Apparently it's upsetting for them to see me more than that. I don't hardly know them any more. I don't think social services should come in and take children away. I think they should have one worker who goes in and helps families rather than separate them straightaway. I think there should be a trial period when someone goes in and helps, say if the mum is an unfit mum, they should help with doing the washing, teaching them how to cook properly and things like that, how to get them to school on time, teaching them how to be a family rather than separate them straightaway.

Residual feelings of being alone and isolated as a result of being in care were frequently described by the young people we spoke to. Sophie, aged 17 at the time of the study, movingly talked about her resistance to telling others about her feelings and how she tended to cope with these on her own:

> I feel like I am totally on my own now, I keep everything to myself. If something is going on in my head, I'll write a letter to myself, I deal with it on my own, because that's how I learned how to deal with it; then I'll read it, cry a bit and then screw the letter up and throw it in the bin.

Building emotional barriers in order to protect themselves from greater rejection and hurt was the coping response adopted by some young people. Miranda explained the effects of care on her in the following way:

> I was not an emotional person before I met my boyfriend because of everything that had happened to me, I put a barrier up around me and somehow he broke the whole barrier down and it wasn't just to him, but now it's like I'm available to the rest of the world as well. Now I have to deal with my emotions again and the fact that I have got feelings means people can hurt them.

Sian, who had had 17 different placements since going into care, felt that she had had to mature early as a result:

> You have to grow up quickly when you are in care. I have been told by my foster mum and dad that I am 18 going on 25…I've had to grow up quick and not have the childhood I should have had.

EXPERIENCES OF SOCIAL CARE WORKERS

Many young people we spoke with not only experienced multiple placements but also had to relate to considerable numbers of social workers, making it difficult to establish any meaningful relationship and rapport with them. Marie commented: 'they [social workers] were always changing…I would just get used to one and then they would leave.'

Sophie expressed some mixed feelings about having a social worker. She explained that, as a result of getting older and because she had been allocated so many different social workers, she no longer found it easy to confide in them:

> I think it is really good to have a social worker; I mean when I was younger it was easier because I could sit there and cry my eyes out and not be embarrassed; and now it's like, well I don't speak to my social worker so much and as you have to change social workers, it's really hard.

Danny, aged 17 when he became a parent, felt very negative about his current social worker. By contrast, he had had a very close relationship with a residential social worker, who he called his 'second mum'. He compared the two:

> My social worker is no help at all – he comes up, says hello, gives me stamps, sorts out a flat and that's it. He's no help at all…a lot of places I've

been, it's like they are just doing their job but with my previous residential worker it was different. She treats me like one of the family. I got invited to her daughter's party and things like that. I still ring her up now and talk to her.

Other young people also described developing a close relationship with a small number of key professionals. The quality of the relationship appeared less related to the professionals' role than to how they conducted themselves when with young people. Those professionals who were most appreciated were reported to take an active interest in a young person, rather than being someone 'just doing their job'. For Ben, the quality of the relationship was also improved by having a sense of fun and enjoyment when spending time with the social worker: 'I did have a social worker...he used to take me from the residential home to the arcades to play pool. I missed working with him...he used to make me laugh and joke...he was cool.'

For Brandon, the ability to communicate with and trust his social worker was what he valued at the core of their relationship: 'I've got a wicked social worker...she's straight with me and talks to me on a level.'

GOING TO SCHOOL

Many of the young people we spoke with had missed a lot of school or had left school at a very young age. David's experience was not untypical: 'I haven't really been to school – haven't been to many because I'd always get kicked out. I couldn't wait to leave.'

Bridget described 'falling into the wrong crowd and skiving off'. Debbie explained how she got expelled the same day she went into care – a sad indictment of the lack of communication and understanding between educational and social care professionals at the time. However, she did acknowledge that she felt that the expulsion was 'totally her fault' (indicative of self-blame) as there were not enough boundaries. She explained that, following the death of her father, she 'pushed and pushed them' and loved the attention it brought.

Brandon spoke angrily and in detail about his lack of education while in care and how this had not only disadvantaged him personally but also, he thought, produced many alienated Black young men:

I left school at 13…this is really what pisses me off…I had troubles at home. I got to school and let a couple of troubles go…so I got kicked out and no other school would take me. Now I'm 16 and they never let no one teach me up until I was 16. They just expect you to get on with it… I was 13 and they left me out. I watch them saying about these young Black men…that they bring guns into this country and they don't do nothing…but basically I'm a Black person born in this country and they didn't do nothing for me, they didn't help me. I was 13, I had a home tutor and she lasted three months and then she had to go about her business. I never got no education. When you fill in that application form and you get to that school bit – I have got nothing to put there…it hurts me that no one gave me that chance to get it… I never got no help.

Dave talked about how he had not been in mainstream education since the age of 11, when he was permanently excluded. From then on he stayed at home and had no tutoring until he went into care at the age of 13. As well as the effect on their educational opportunities that moving around had on young people, several also described the stigma that they experienced within education as a result of entering a school while being in local authority care. Liz, for example, aged 16 and pregnant with her first baby, described the response she received when starting a new school as a result of a placement move. 'One of the teachers said, "I suppose you'll need special needs being in care and everything"… It was just because I was a foster child, they think you can't be good.'

In the same vein, one foster carer who had looked after many young people in her care talked about some of the complexities of keeping foster care children in education and the stigma that surrounded them:

The majority that come to me have missed school, have low educational attainment and are often 'statemented'. The local school doesn't want to take them, they are prejudiced because they are a child in care. It's very hard to get any education for them, even five hours a week with home tutors.

CONCLUSIONS

One of the aims of this book is to question views that regard teenage pregnancy as no more than a problem to be avoided. However, much of this chapter has highlighted quite negative aspects of young people's entry into and experience of the care system, often characterised by relationship breakdown, rejection, abandonment, abuse and instability. Given these early adversities, it may seem difficult to imagine how many of these young people would be able to successfully parent their own children. Later chapters, however, show how, despite their difficult and often traumatic start in life, many young people could change and, to a degree, improve their lives, when they or their partners were pregnant or when they became parents. Wanting their children's lives to be different from their own – and being provided with the means to achieve this – assisted young people to develop a strong sense of themselves as good enough parents.

The lessons to be learned from young people's accounts of their experiences of family life and care are not necessarily complex: the young people who spoke with us needed to feel safe, secure and loved. A number of them, for example, had experienced violence and had often witnessed it too. Many had been moved from one care placement to another, often with little or no preparation or introduction to their new 'families'. The young people repeatedly expressed how they wanted to establish relationships with carers and other professionals who listened to them, responded to what they said and so build a sense of mutual understanding and trust.

However, knowing what young people need is somewhat different from actually providing them with safe and supportive environments that nurture their confidence and esteem and help them to do their best as they make the transition to parenthood. In the following chapters, we first outline the ways that young people learned about sex and relationships and then report on what they told us about their experiences of pregnancy and parenthood.

CHAPTER 4

GOING IT ALONE: YOUNG PEOPLE'S EXPERIENCES OF LEARNING ABOUT SEX AND RELATIONSHIPS

More young people need more advice about safe sex and that. Like, I didn't really know nothing and I know I've been stupid. It would have been better if they'd done some of this stuff in the children's homes. There was nothing.

INTRODUCTION

In this chapter, we highlight what young people said with regard to learning about sex and relationships as well as their experiences accessing sexual health services. More often than not, the young people who spoke with us stated that they had had few opportunities to learn about sex from adults – whether from their birth parents, residential or foster carers, social workers, teachers or professionals in sexual health services. One result of this was that some young people, at least, were left confused or anxious about sex, and others appeared rather sceptical or distrustful of services providing education about sex or sexual health services. That said, some young people provided suggestions about how to improve their own and others, access to information, advice and guidance on sex, relationships and sexual health.

YOUNG PEOPLE'S UNCERTAINTIES
ABOUT SEX AND CONCEPTION

Most of the young people we spoke with commented on their lack of opportunities to learn about sex and sex-related issues as well as sexual relationships. Some young people mentioned that the lack of timely, relevant and trustworthy provision led to friends becoming a necessary, if limited, source of information. Penny, who was aged 16 and pregnant with her first child when she spoke to us, said:

> I didn't really learn much at all from school, they didn't do much on it and they weren't really interested. Most of what I've learned, I've learned myself with friends, I know all about sex and contraception...I think it's important that they do more on the emotional side of things.

For many young people, learning about sex was largely experiential in the sense that they reported having sex before they really knew anything about it. Jack, who was 23 years old and had a four-year-old daughter, reflected on how he attempted to learn more about sex and the basic physiology of men and women through watching pornography – a source of information also cited by a number of other young people who spoke to us: 'I lost my virginity at 14 but I did not talk about things like that with anyone. I watched my dad's porno videos to learn about this three hole, two hole story.' Serena commented: 'I started having sex when I was 13. All my mates were doing it and I didn't want to be the only one left out. They were all saying how good it was.'

However, the lack of information about sex and relationships appeared to lead many young people to feel that they were on their own on this matter. Some young people had made particular efforts to find out about sex – although they recognised that working it out for themselves was not necessarily the best of way accessing or having accurate information. Jenny, who was 15 years old and had a son who was just a few months old, commented: 'I had to find out for myself...so most probably got it a bit wrong because I had to find out for myself.'

Catherine, who was 20 years old, having had her son at 18, reflected that if she had known more about relationships she might have had a more equal relationship with her ex-partner:

> If I treated his dad a bit more meaner and wasn't so nice – he was older than
> me, 35 and I was 18 – there wouldn't have been so much drama going on
> between us. I was such a simple person. I didn't say anything, I didn't argue.

For young men, finding out oneself about sex seemed particularly common, even if becoming *streetwise* in this domain at least was a somewhat serendipitous experience. Timothy, who was 21 when he spoke with us and had three children, the first when he was 16 years old, commented: 'I went to a Catholic school and never had any sex education. I learned by trial and error on the streets.'

Whether or not information and guidance about sex and relationships was or was not available to them, many young people described a hesitancy in accessing information, preferring instead to sort things out for themselves and 'go it alone'. Siobhan, who was pregnant for the first time when she spoke to us, said: 'I don't really like talking to people outside our families. I don't trust other people easily as they are strangers and I don't like talking in groups…and not about sensitive stuff.'

As well as stating that they had little or inaccurate information about sex-related issues, a number of young people also reported being confused about their own experiences. In Chapter 2, for example, Amanda described how she was terrified at the point when she started menstruating and felt completely unprepared and ignorant of what was happening to her. Similarly Anna, who was 18 and had a 10-month-old daughter, said:

> It would have been good to have someone to talk to 'cos I probably
> wouldn't have got in this sort of mess. My mum didn't sit me down and tell
> me about my periods and how they worked… that's why I got pregnant… I
> never actually understood periods, they just came and went.

David was 18 and had a one-year-old daughter when he spoke with us. His confusion about conception became apparent when he was asked whether he was surprised that he had not got a girl pregnant as he had not been using contraception. He replied: 'No, because you can't get a girl pregnant at 13. Don't you have to be a certain age before you can get a girl pregnant?'

For most young people, birth families played only a very small part in informing them about sex and relationships. In fact, of all the young people who spoke with us, only five of them reported family members taking on this role. Some young people were critical about receiving such information from their birth mothers, saying that it was carried out either inappropriately or at too young an age. Karen, who was 16 and had a one-year-old daughter, said:

> I learned about sex from my mother at the age of three...which probably didn't help the fact that I got pregnant so early. I used to be scared of saying the word sex and she used to make me say it. On the one hand it might be good at a young age but not that young!

LEARNING ABOUT SEX AND RELATIONSHIPS

On the whole, young people indicated that they had not been involved in discussions about sex and relationships with adults. Only six of the young women interviewed indicated that residential workers had talked to them about sex and relationships. One young man – who had been looked after all his life – stated that his foster carer had never talked to him about sex, contraception and relationships. Moreover, only one young person said her social worker had provided her with this kind of information, and only one young person said the same about her leaving care social worker.

Although some of the young people who were interviewed reported having received information about sex, contraception and relationships in residential care, there were many more who felt that the information given was either non-existent or inadequate. As Amy, aged 18 and mother of a three-year-old son, argued:

> I think one of the reasons so many girls got pregnant in care was that there was not enough information about contraception in the homes. The staff never talked to us about it, I think they were a bit embarrassed. We did use to have girls' nights, I used to love those, we used to sit and pamper ourselves and talk with the workers about boys, but we didn't talk about sex and contraception. They could have spoken to us at the children's meetings we had once a month.

David also felt strongly that a lot more should be done by children's homes:

> More young people need more advice about safe sex and that. Like, I didn't really know nothing and I know I've been stupid. It would have been better

> if they'd done some of this stuff in the children's homes. There was nothing. Even if they just said you could talk to them about it or if they left some of the booklets around. We needed more advice on sex, contraception and relationships too.

With regard to foster care, some young people, mainly young women, reported difficulties in talking to their foster carers about sex and contraception, often thinking that they would not approve. Donna, who was 18 when she spoke with us, having had her son when she was 17, said: 'They didn't tell me anything. They didn't think I was the type to have sex early, I think it would have been embarrassing for them and me.'

Georgia, who had the first of her three children at the age of 14, described a clash of values and beliefs between herself and her foster carers as a reason why she could not use a form of contraception:

> The Pill was a big no-no in my foster carers' house. If they found out I was on the Pill, they would know I was having sex and they would be disgusted and I didn't want them to make me feel like that.

Lisa, who had also been pregnant for the first time at 14, said that she had simply been 'warned' by her foster carers 'to be careful', but that the information given was all too vague: 'Like one of the carers, she would tell me to be "careful", but at that time I didn't know what she meant.'

As well as commenting on sex education from residential and foster carers, young people also spoke about schools. They highlighted that sex education should be timely and relevant as well as taught, with humour, through discussion by skilled adults. Tamsin was aged 20 and had a two-year-old son when she spoke with us. Although she had moved from one school to another and missed out on sex education lessons, she echoed the sentiments of others that, to be useful, sex education had, at least, to be timely. 'I moved schools, so missed out then…because they had already covered it. I'd been having relationships for ages by then'.

While a number of young people noted that they had already begun sexual relationships by the time they were provided with sex education, Georgia had already had her first child: 'I knew nothing before I had sex for the first time. They did do sex education at school, but that was too late, I had already had my baby!'

For Amanda, it was the actual birth of her daughter when she was 16 that first appeared to prompt others to talk to her about using contraception: 'The only time that I ever got information was after I had had the baby. Everyone was saying make sure you go on the Pill so that you don't have another baby…that was a bit late then.'

While the timeliness of sex education was raised as an issue, so too was its relevance – particularly that provided in schools. The content of lessons, for example, was rarely seen to be pertinent to young people. It often lacked opportunities for young people to learn about relationships or was too focused on some biological issues while omitting others. Serena, who was 19 years old when she spoke with us, having had her son at the age of 17, said: 'At school, sex ed. was crap. All we learned at school was about periods and hormones. They didn't teach you anything about HIV/STIs [sexually transmitted infections] or relationships.'

Not being given full information about different forms of contraception and about being a mother was seen by some young people, particularly young women, to be a significant gap in what they had learned. Serena commented: 'All you get told is about when you start your periods. You don't get told about the Pill or having a baby, just about the condom and that's it.'

Serena commented that a better understanding of pregnancy and motherhood might also be useful for young people to develop: 'I think there should be more of those virtual babies in school and wearing the empathy belly so young girls know what it might be like.'[1]

Young people also commented on the style in which sex education was taught. Too great a use was made, for example, of written information. While some young people found leaflets and posters to be of use, an over-reliance on them was also felt to be an inadequate method of sex education. Dave, who had the first of his four children at 15, said:

> I think leaflets and things like that don't fully explain things properly. I think most people know what sex is and how to do it and that, but it's the things that happen afterwards that people don't understand [referring to STIs and pregnancy].

---

1   The 'empathy belly' is a weighted garment that aims to encourage young people to understand better the physical experiences of pregnancy. See, for example, BBC News Online (2000) and www.empathybelly.org/home.html, accessed on 5 April 2008.

When talking with friends about sex, some people noted that they did so with humour, by 'having a laugh'. Sex education was too often taught, some young people suggested, too seriously – which led young people to disregard much of what was taught. Sonia was 18 and had a one-year-old daughter. She commented: 'I think a lot of young people don't take much notice of what they're told and don't take it seriously because it's in a group and young people want a laugh'.

The use of humour was said to be one of the characteristics of more successful forms of sex education. Another was that those teaching it should know how to do so with young people – a skill that some teachers were not necessarily seen to hold but which an educator in their 20s might possess. Debbie, who had just turned 17 and was nine months' pregnant when she spoke with us, said:

> Sex and relationships should be taught by someone younger who knows something about children and who works with teenagers. We all know the people that get across to teenagers and the people who don't...I don't think the teacher should do it. It should be done by someone in the 20s, someone that young people will listen to, and they've got to make it fun...
> It is too serious.

The need for educators skilled in enabling young people to learn about sex and relationships appeared important for young people in general and especially so for a smaller number of young people we spoke with, in particular, who had learning difficulties – often linked to language and communication. For Lisa, learning about sex and relationships had proved particularly difficult and she was left wondering whether her lack of knowledge or understanding was due to a fault of hers, or to the limitations of others. Jasmine, who said that she had attention deficit hyperactivity disorder (ADHD), commented on how she would talk about relationships only to people who she knew well and 'I would make sure I trust them'.

As well as talking with us about their experiences of learning about sex and relationships, where they had done so, a few young people also commented on their experiences of using sexual health services. Particularly important to young people was 'confidentiality'. They stated that they would use services on the basis that 'They don't give out information to anyone'.

Some services were found to have been intrusive and embarrassing. Some young men, for example, reported being asked what they perceived to be personal questions when they were picking up condoms. Ben was 18 and had the first of his three children at 16. Although he knew that he could obtain condoms free of charge through some services, he commented:

> I just buy condoms 'cos it's quicker and easier and you don't have to talk to people at all. When I was about 15, I went to a clinic and got lots of condoms...someone was talking to me for about 20 minutes (!) and I just wanted condoms.

Although young people were generally critical about the opportunities made available to them to discuss, talk and learn about sex and relationships, when this did happen it was commented on favourably. Those few young people who indicated that they had been provided with information about sex within their residential home or supported accommodation were, on the whole, positive about the quality and relevance of the information they had received. Lucy, who was 17 when she spoke with us and had her son when she was 16, said:

> The manager of the supported housing unit told us about contraception. She sat the girls down and told us we should have the coil, the Pill or depo [contraceptive injection] and explained it all to us. She talked about STDs [sexually transmitted diseases] and stuff too...she did this every time there were new girls in the home.

USE OF CONTRACEPTION

We asked young people to talk about their use of contraception – either before they or their partner first became pregnant, or their current use. With regard to the first pregnancy, almost all young people stated that they either had not used any form of contraception, or had done so irregularly. A few stated that they had experienced a failure in contraception.

One of the most common reasons for not using contraception, either at all or only on an irregular basis, was a reported dislike of condoms. Both young men and young women mentioned this. Janet, who was 16 and pregnant with her first child, said: 'I don't like condoms as it does feel different! My partner also didn't like the feeling.' Ben shared this view of condoms: 'I don't wear condoms as I don't like wearing them. I don't get any pleasure.'

Young men and women also indicated that they thought that pregnancy would not happen to them. Sonia said: 'We were using condoms, but only sometimes, but I thought it wouldn't happen to me.' Steve, who was aged 20 and had a one-year-old son, said: 'Condoms do not feel comfortable and I prefer to get away with not using anything. We didn't consider that she'd get pregnant really but we'd only had sex three times when she got pregnant.'

Many of the young women spoke in terms of getting 'caught out'. This often occurred in the context of not having conceived after a long period of unprotected sex, with the result that they felt they were somehow immune. Phoebe, aged 20 and pregnant with her second child, said: 'I wasn't using anything for a long time – I had never got caught before.'

A few young women indicated that they felt unable to ask a partner to use a condom. Sonia, for example, stated:

> I first found out about sex with my first boyfriend at 15. I knew a bit about sex from school and I knew about condoms but it's hard when you are young to ask someone to use one… I think it's easier when you are older. Now I feel more confident about it.

Other reasons for not using contraception included problems experienced in the past with certain forms of contraception. One young man, for example, spoke about his girlfriend's allergy to condoms and several young women reported side effects of hormonal contraception, such as weight gain and mood changes from injectable contraceptives as well as the Pill.

Many of the young women who were interviewed also reported 'forgetting' to take the Pill. Karen, who was 16 when we spoke with her, having had her daughter at the age of 15, said: 'I was on the Pill but I kept missing it…I'd wake up and have the whole day and just forget.'

Some also reported having problems in obtaining repeat prescriptions for the Pill, especially when there were frequent changes of carers, placements and GPs. Poppy was 20 years old, had her first child when she was 17 and when we spoke with her was pregnant with her second child. She described in detail some of the logistical and other barriers to regular contraceptive use:

> I should have gone on the Pill, but because of my weight and because I smoke I can't go on a Pill that's more easily available. I have to go through the doctors, but because I was moving around so much I didn't have a set doctor. I should have made more of an effort to sort it out. But you don't. When you're 16 or 17 you don't think 'Oh this might happen or that might happen'.

Of those who experienced a failure of a chosen contraceptive method, one of the main reasons given for this was split condoms. Julia, who was 16 and pregnant with her first baby, reflected: 'The condom split but we thought nothing of it. It was a "one-off" – we thought nothing of it.'

Other young women reported being sick or taking antibiotics while on the Pill, therefore reducing its efficacy. They also said that they did not know that these factors could affect the reliability of the Pill as a contraceptive, and felt that they should have been given more information. Such was the case with Amy, who stated: 'I was on the Pill at the time, but was taking antibiotics which affected it. I wish someone had told me.'

A few young women reported using contraception correctly, whether it was the Pill, contraceptive injection or condoms, but had the experience of it still failing, resulting in an unplanned pregnancy. Emergency contraception, however, was mentioned only by a couple of the young people who spoke with us.

PROFESSIONALS' PERSPECTIVES: A DIFFICULT ISSUE TO PRIORITISE

Professionals generally recognised the importance of providing young people with information, and engaging them in discussions, about sex and relationships. Some professionals noted that young people's experiences of health services more generally affected how they felt about accessing services related to sexual health.

Many professionals, for example, spoke of young people's dislike of the annual medical examinations they were expected to comply with. These, they felt, created a barrier to discussing health in general, including sexual health. As one leaving care manager commented: 'Often they refuse to take part and why not since every other young person they know of only consults a doctor or health worker as and when the need arises.'

Another manager said of 'boarding out' medicals:

> I have accompanied them [the young people] and I wouldn't want them done to me. They can be particularly embarrassing to young women – questions can be very intrusive. They have been in care because they have been abused and yet they are subjected to this. It's like being a car having an MOT [test of roadworthiness] – but we're not talking about cars but about children.

With regard, more specifically, to sex education, professionals recognised that, if provided at all, such education from birth families could be inaccurate or inconsistent. Some professionals stressed the importance of providing looked after young people with consistent messages, particularly if many different professionals were involved in their care. A coordinator of an education team for looked after young people stated:

> Although lots of different professionals and lay people have a role to play, it is important that kids get consistent messages. It is important that we don't fail the kids in care and as corporate parents we need to aim to offer them the same standard of care and advice on sex and relationships other kids get from their own parents.

Most professionals indicated that the responsibility for conversations and education about sex lay with adults who had day-to-day and face-to-face contact with young people in care – and especially with the adult with whom the young person felt most comfortable. As one voluntary project development worker stated: 'It should come down to who the young person feels most comfortable with…it should come down to everybody. It should be there across the board.'

There was felt to be a collective and corporate responsibility among professionals and families for ensuring that conversations and discussions about sex and relationships actually took place. About half of the professionals interviewed felt that the social worker or leaving care social worker should take a lead in talking to young people about sex and relationships. One manager of a residential home stated: 'Personally I think it's a collective responsibility between the parents and whoever the carer of the young person is going to be, the social worker, a foster carer, a care worker in residential and the schools.'

Even though professionals were generally agreed that issues related to sex and relationships should be discussed with young people, they recognised that there were a number of barriers to doing so. Some challenges, for example, lay in the frequency with which young people were moved around in residential care, while others related to the perceived nature and purpose of residential care itself.

One family support worker, who carried out a lot of face-to-face work with looked after young people, including education about sex and relationships, spoke about the difficulties of moving around frequently, and the impact this had on young people accessing information and services:

> In reality, I think positive relationships are harder to build as many young people move and don't stay in one place long enough to build relationships in foster or residential care. If they were able to build relationships better with their carers, I feel a lot of information could be shared through these relationships.

In one of the study sites, all the residential homes for children and young people had been closed, and in another the future of residential children's homes, and whether or not they would continue to be a placement option, was very unclear. This uncertainty about the status of residential care was seen as one of the reasons why fundamentals like health and sex education were not always addressed, as they should be. One deputy manager of a residential children's home explained:

> It becomes difficult to grasp what the purpose of a children's home is and that means that the general environment that young people are living in is hectic, chaotic and unstable. And so it's difficult to allocate time, make time for positive interactive sessions and actually share and discuss information and allow young people to digest that information and go away and benefit from it.

Another challenge identified by respondents, related to the priority given to sex education. As one professional stated, there often seemed to be other, more pressing problems, to address – such as the use of alcohol and drugs and petty crime. One services manager for looked after children said:

> We wait for young people to make us aware for example of mental health or pregnancy then we access the service. We need to be more active in accessing services before we need them…a lot of the time we do things in crisis.

A senior practitioner in a leaving care team explained that sex and sexual health is often not seen as a priority, due to other more pressing problems: 'Sexual health realistically would come quite a long way down the list for me. If someone is homeless and has got no money then those things are going to be tackled as the main priorities.'

A number of professionals noted that foster carers had a particular role to play in providing education about sex and relationships. As most social workers did not have enough day-to-day contact with the young person to be able to address these issues effectively, this needed to be done by the young person's main carer. One nurse specialist for looked after children noted that in the central England research site in which she worked, around 90 per cent of looked after young people would have had experience of foster care and stated: 'We have an enormous responsibility to empower foster carers in order that they can empower young people.'

However, some professionals also acknowledged that there might be particular challenges in expecting foster carers to involve young people in discussions about sex and relationships. In the London research site in particular, for example, some foster carers were said to hold strong religious beliefs which might make it difficult for them to talk with young people about having sex before marriage. One foster care manager talked about how some foster carers were uncomfortable discussing the use of tampons rather than sanitary towels with young women, because the foster carer thought it would affect young women's 'virginity'.

In the central England research site, the nurse specialist for looked after children went on to discuss some of the practical difficulties in encouraging foster carers to access available training to educate and support young people about sex, contraception and relationships:

> We had three training events for foster carers, but they were cancelled because we only had a couple of people who wanted to take part. Foster carers are inundated with training. They are not paid to go on training so I

don't think they are going to attend unless it is a particular issue for them at a given time. It may be that we need to start looking at it in a different way.

Some foster carers, themselves, also raised problems resulting from the lack of clarity about the role of talking to young people about sex and relationships. As one foster carer noted:

> Sometimes they will have their parents around so it's not your responsibility as the carer, and it depends on who they want to talk to. In reality, some don't want to hear because some kids look at it as that you're not their parents so you can't tell them what to do.

Taken together, the views and experiences of a range of professionals indicate that responsibility for sex education was somewhat diffuse among adults looking after young people, with the result that the provision of sex education could be overlooked. Training, guidance and assistance to help professionals to involve young people in discussions about sex and relationships appeared patchy. Having said this, in three of the sites in which the study took place, professionals reported that much had been done to improve the provision of training and support to professionals and carers and to provide clearer policy and guidance. One social services manager for looked after children said:

> In terms of the whole area of SRE [sex and relationships education] work, it's growing, it's difficult, it's slow, it's a drip, drip effect but it has come an awfully long way. I think there is a genuine desire to access training and real difficulties to do this brought about by staff shortages. We are continuously trying to make it a part of people's appraisal and development programmes and also being more imaginative in how we take it [training] out...progress is frustratingly slow but it is there.

CONCLUSIONS

In this chapter, we have highlighted the limited role that education about sex and relationships had in the lives of young people in and from care. Some young people stated that they had been particularly anxious about some aspects of their physical development, sex and conception – such as menstruation. Others stated that more could be done to make sex education timely and relevant to them. Young people suggested that adults needed not only to talk about sex and relationships with them with little or no embarrassment, but also to do so with humour. For those young people with learning difficulties, particular attention needed to be paid to the process and content of education.

While professionals, on the one hand, recognised that young people needed to learn about sex and relationships, they appeared, on the other hand, to struggle to make this a priority. They suggested that those professionals who had a day-to-day contact with young people in care – such as residential and foster carers – might be best placed to involve young people in discussions about sex and relationships yet acknowledged also that there might be particular challenges for foster carers in particular to take on this role. Indeed, while occasionally commenting favourably on the limited sex education provided in residential care, young people were rather more ambivalent or negative when it came to foster carers, who they felt could be more likely to let their personal values get in the way of them providing them with the information and guidance about sex and relationships that they needed.

However, one aim of this chapter is to highlight that, perhaps as with young people in general, young people in and from care too often have limited opportunities to engage with good quality discussions and education regarding sex and relationships. Such education is, in and of itself, an important entitlement for young people to learn about their (and other's) bodies, emotions and relationships. While it may have a place in preventing teenage conceptions, it should perhaps be seen, rather more broadly, as one aspect of providing a rounded education for and with young people. As we highlight in the following chapters, when young people in care spoke about the factors they associated with pregnancy and parenthood, these were not solely related to their levels of knowledge about sex and contraception.

CHAPTER 5

DECIDING WHAT TO DO: YOUNG PEOPLE'S REACTIONS AND RESPONSES TO PREGNANCY

I was shocked, utterly and completely.
It hit me like a ton of bricks.

INTRODUCTION

'Planning' a pregnancy is a complex notion for many men and women, regardless of whether they are young or somewhat older. People may plan their pregnancy in different ways too – sometimes carefully with a great deal of forethought, and at other times much less systematically. Only a few young people we spoke with told us that they had consciously planned their pregnancy. Most, however, had not, and just a few said that, while they had not planned it, neither did they actively attempt to prevent it.

Although some young people had stopped using contraception and knew that there was an increased risk of pregnancy, they did not necessarily want to have a child straightaway. James, who at the age of 18 was about to become a father, explained: 'My girlfriend was on the Pill, but when she stopped we knew that she may get pregnant but both of us had talked about having a child at some point, so it wasn't a massive issue.'

Finding out about a pregnancy provoked some anxiety for most young people as they had to contend with a challenging combination of their own emotions, the responses of partners as well as the reactions of family members (either birth or foster families) all of whom were involved, to varying degrees, in their lives. Importantly, many young people described how they could almost predict the response they would receive from significant others when they told them they were pregnant, as these reactions tended to reflect the type of relationships they already had with them. Volatile reactions to the pregnancy, for example, tended to typify the stormy relationship they already had with partners or family. Similarly, indifference, empathy, happiness, pragmatism and concern were all responses that tended to echo existing relationships with significant others.

As discussed earlier, most young people were not using contraception on a regular basis at the time when they became pregnant. Despite this fact, the most common reaction to pregnancy for both young women and young men was one of 'shock', a word used repeatedly in our discussions with them. Susie, who had a baby at age 17, reacted to the news that she was pregnant in the following way: 'I was shocked, I was speechless. Water was coming out of my eyes and I didn't know what to say. I didn't know what to do.'

Poppy, aged 17 when her first child was born, said: 'I was shocked, utterly and completely. It hit me like a ton of bricks. I was in complete and utter denial. I just couldn't get my head around it.'

Amy was 15 and living in a residential children's home when she discovered she was pregnant. Her initial reaction was also typical of many of the young women we spoke to:

> I was devastated. I was young and was in shock… I was in care and me and a friend took a pregnancy test for a laugh and just my luck, she wasn't pregnant but I was! I didn't think it would happen to me!

Shock and surprise, however, were often also accompanied by more positive emotions. Colleen and Penny described some of these in response to hearing that they were pregnant. Colleen said:

> At first I thought it might just be the Pill messing my periods up but when I actually found out I was, I thought 'Oh my God it can't be, it can't be me, I'm too young'. It upset me a bit when I did the home test, it wasn't planned,

but I thought I'll just get on with it. I did three home tests at first, it was such a shock, I kept thinking that each one must be wrong. It took about a week, two weeks to actually get used to the idea but then I was quite pleased. I was like 'Wow, I'm gonna have a baby'.

Penny said:

A friend of my mum's (I think she's got a bit of gypsy in her or something – she's old and wise), she knew before I did. She said you're pregnant and I said, 'Don't be stupid'…but when I did find out I was in shock, it was unplanned. It was like an accident. I didn't come on for about six days, I'm not normally late but I thought, 'Oh well I'll take a test then'. I'm never late unless I'm having a really bad month and the stress stops it coming for a couple of days. I said to my boyfriend that we needed to do a pregnancy test but we couldn't do it at first because his dad was over from Spain and he doesn't get to see him a lot so we waited until after. I was kind of excited about it… I was like 'I'm keeping it, I want to keep it' but I hadn't really thought about it, the responsibility or anything like that. Yeah, we both knew it was a possibility, but we were still shocked when it happened, it hit me, 'I really am gonna be a mum'.

Young men described similarly mixed reactions to the news that they were about to become parents. A number of them talked of how their first response to being told about the pregnancy was one of denial that the baby was theirs. Dave, for instance, who was 15 when his partner at the time was pregnant with his first child, said:

I'd been told that she was pregnant but I denied it was mine. But I knew it was mine really. But I was just a child myself so I didn't want to have one. I was a bit stupid then and didn't really care about anything.

Some young men said they were quite happy about the news of their partner's pregnancy, but others were worried about how they were going to financially support the mother and their child. Many felt they were not old enough to take on such responsibilities. Alex became a parent at the age of 16 and described his reaction when he found out about the pregnancy: 'I shit myself. I wasn't ready to be a dad.'

Like the young women, many young men expressed ambivalent feelings. Steve was 19 when his partner, then 16, discovered that she was pregnant. He commented: 'My girlfriend phoned me and asked me if she could come over… She told me and I was surprised and shit scared and I am still getting used to the idea of being a parent.'

For Ian, age 17 and waiting for the arrival of his first baby, the news of the pregnancy provoked not only ambivalent feelings and concern about being able to support his girlfriend and baby but also a change of attitude and behaviour:

> I'd been sniffing glue and my girlfriend came to where I was staying and told me to put my hand out and she put the pregnancy test in my hand and said, 'You are going to be a dad'. I got this most sickly feeling and said to myself, 'Now is the time to stop sniffing' and I did from them on. Half of me was happy but the other half was sad. I was thinking, 'How am I going to able to support her?' All thoughts fell from my head but I was happy as I'd always wanted to be a dad but didn't realise it would be at a young age.

For many of the young people, their reactions to the pregnancy were different a few days after the initial news. Karen, aged 15 when she had her first baby, vividly described a mixture of emotions, with the reality of being a mother being far from her consciousness:

> I felt happy, peed off…everything… I felt everything…a couple of days…the horrible side of the emotions…not wanting anything to do with the baby. It didn't sink in until two or three days later…when I first heard I was on a high…then I thought I was giving birth to a doll or something possibly… I probably didn't understand that you had to look after it and feed it and bathe it and clothe it and the rest of it.

Sophie, who at 17 was pregnant with her first baby, was initially delighted about the pregnancy:

> I was chuffed; I wanted a baby for ages… I don't know whether that's common. I've always wanted a baby. You know how people have dreams, oh I want to be a businessman, I want to be…my dream was, all I want is to have a baby. I was so happy, I couldn't stop crying.

As soon as she had told everyone, and everyone had congratulated her, she felt a little differently about the prospect of becoming a parent. Like many other young people we spoke with, much of her anxiety related to her age and the fact that imminent motherhood would signify a transition from childhood to adulthood, clearly a shift that she was grappling with:

Sometimes I think, I shouldn't be having a baby, I am only a kid myself; but then other times I think, OK, I was only a kid six months ago, now I am an adult, I need to be an adult… Some people have said I have missed out on my childhood – OK, but I have chosen, I don't want my childhood. But I think fuck it, I can still have a good time with the baby, people go out all the time, on weekends, you just have to feel comfortable to leave your child… I'll be 18, I am only supposed to go out then.

REACTIONS OF PARTNERS

The initial reaction of young women's partners when learning about a pregnancy was often of 'shock' and 'surprise'. However, these feelings were frequently also accompanied by concern and anxiety regarding their own and their girlfriend's age, where the money needed would come from and the responsibility involved in becoming a parent. Colleen's partner, for example, was concerned about both their ages and whether it was the right time to become parents:

My boyfriend was there with me and he read the test before me, he said, 'You've got to go to the doctor, you're pregnant'. We'd been going out about nine months I think. He wanted to be there with me. After we knew for sure we got back and my boyfriend said, 'I don't think this is the best idea because we are still so young, I don't think I'm ready to be a dad yet'.

Rather than concern, the reaction of Fran's partner was one of anger:

He [my partner] was angry and he wanted me to get rid of it and we split up after it because I wouldn't get rid of it…then got back together again later because he realised that I was definitely keeping it. He wanted to be there and see her and that but he got deported at the end of May…so she hasn't seen her dad.

Georgia already had one daughter when she discovered, aged 15, that she was about to have her second child. She described how although she hoped things would work out with her partner at the time, she found herself involved in a very violent relationship with him, which ultimately put herself and her daughter at risk. She explained:

I was really pleased… I was with his dad, but it didn't work out…he was really obsessive, he slit his throat in front of us, he tried to jump off a bridge; it was all in the papers and all that, he threatened to kill me and my daughter.

Karen, pregnant at age 16, described a similar experience after telling her partner about the pregnancy: 'He punched me in my stomach and tried to kill me so I don't think he was very happy about it…it sunk in afterwards and then he was happy about it…but the punch could have killed it already.'

These more violent reactions from partners is a theme that we return to in later chapters in this book since it impacted in various ways on the lives of some young parents who spoke with us. Such extreme reactions aside, there were many examples where partners were reportedly supportive and helpful once the initial shock of the pregnancy had subsided. Young women variably described how partners would buy them foods that they craved for, ensured that they had all the necessary equipment for the baby and supported them emotionally throughout the pregnancy.

REACTIONS OF RELATIVES

In general, the reactions of some family members tended to be more negative than those of partners. Young women's mothers, in particular, often considered their daughters too young to have a baby and consequently encouraged them to terminate the pregnancy. Fran spoke about her mother's negative reaction to the news of the pregnancy: 'My mum said to have an abortion because I was too young… I said I was going to keep it.'

Amy was 14 when she became pregnant and was living in a children's home. She experienced a shocked response from her mother: 'She [my mum] stopped speaking to me for about three months. The staff phoned her when I told them I was pregnant and she cried her eyes out.'

Sonia contrasted her mother's initial negative response to her father's: 'My mum told me to get rid of it and my dad was happy about it…my mum changed her attitude later.'

Worrying about the reactions of their parents was frequently described as the overriding concern once a pregnancy was confirmed. Mandy described how she was taken for a pregnancy test by a worker in the residential care home where she was living. Her first thought, she said, when she found out the result, was 'Me mum is gonna kill us', and her second, 'Me dad would strangle us'. Similarly, Katie's initial thoughts were about her mother's response:

My first reaction was 'What will me mum think?' ...that was the first thing I thought of...because she's my mum and I thought I was going to get told off ...and forced to have an abortion and all that.

Rosie, like other young people with no really close family ties, was somewhat at a loss as to who to share her news with. Having left the home of her adoptive parents at 16 and having only had sporadic contact with her birth mother, Rosie said:

I told my mum but she didn't really want to know, she thought I was stupid. She sort of said don't talk to me about it... I couldn't tell my dad 'cos I didn't know where he was. I didn't really have any contact with my adopted brothers and sisters neither. My stepbrother – I didn't see him because my mum wouldn't let me...so there was no one really.

Yet not all of the young women's birth mothers and fathers were negative at learning that they were to become grandparents. In some cases, despite anxieties, sometimes based on their own personal experiences, of how their daughters would cope, some parents reacted in measured and supportive ways. Colleen, for example, described her relief at the reaction from various family members:

I was quite surprised that my dad didn't try to influence me in any way. I think his first words were, 'There's no point crying over spilt milk', he was a bit shocked, I'm his little girl. He was quite supportive, I thought he was going to shout and everything but he didn't even start to raise his voice. I was quite shocked, more shocked about that than being pregnant! I was really worried about telling him, my boyfriend told him, 'We've got something to tell you, C's pregnant'. I was quite worried about telling my mum as well. I didn't live with her at the time, but the time before when I was there we were talking about pregnancy and at the time I had no idea I was pregnant and she was like 'try not to get pregnant too early' because she had done. She was about 18 when she had my older brother and, although she doesn't regret it, she say's it was hard. They was all a bit worried 'cos I'm so young I might not be able to cope and that, but otherwise they gave me their full support and they weren't angry with me.

Liz's sister and mother were also supportive:

My sister spoke to me at first and said, 'Are you sure you want it, you know it's a big step'. I said, 'I'm not sure'. She said, 'Well you've got a bit of time to decide', and she said, 'Whatever you decide, I am there for you'. My mum come down and said, 'If you don't want it, it's not fair to keep it, I don't believe in abortion, but I will stand by you whatever you decide'. She has been hard on me, asking me how I am going to cope, asking me if I want nappies, what am I going to get… Harsh about the realities of having a baby. My mother had her first baby at 14, so she knows what she's talking about.

In some instances, becoming pregnant at an early age actually reunited estranged birth parents and their children, as Claire explained:

My dad actually told my mum [about the pregnancy] as me and my mum weren't talking at the time; and it actually brought us together. She opened her door with open arms; which surprised me, because I hadn't talked to her for two years.

DECIDING WHAT TO DO

Less than half of the young women interviewed reported receiving help from anyone at all in considering the options open to them with respect to their pregnancy. Rosie, with practically no contact or links with family members, commented: 'I made all the decisions myself.'

Where they did receive advice and support from services in making their decisions, young people were most likely to identify youth services or health clinics as the best sources of information and support. Privacy and confidentiality were the most important criteria for young people when they considered accessing or using these services.

Foster carers were also mentioned as sometimes being helpful, although a small number of young women felt they could not talk to their foster carers about their pregnancies because they were worried about potential disapproval. Jenny, who was 15 when she became pregnant, talked of how she felt under no pressure from her foster mother to make any particular decision: 'My foster Mum gave me all the options to choose from…but she didn't persuade me to do anything…I wasn't pushed in any particular direction.'

Simone, aged 22 at the time of the research, was 15 years old and living in foster care when she became pregnant with the first of her two children. She had been living with her foster mother for only about a year and described how awkward it was for her to discuss the pregnancy and consider the options with her: 'It was difficult – I wanted to tell my foster Mum, but I didn't know how she would feel. I felt like she was still a stranger to me, I didn't know how she would react.'

One foster carer we spoke with described the dilemma faced by many looked after young women: 'One young mum I was looking after didn't tell me she was pregnant because she knew I loved children so much and thought I would be against her having an abortion.'

In fact, a few young people reported their foster carers persuading them not to have an abortion. As Susie explained: 'My foster mum told me not to get rid of it, 'cos she's not going to advise me to get an abortion because she had her baby at 17 and that really helped me.'

With a few exceptions, young women were most likely to report that they felt pressurised into having a termination rather than being helped to make their own, informed, decisions. The pressure to have an abortion was most likely to come from mothers and boyfriends, despite the fact that many young men taking part in the current study expressed strong anti-abortion attitudes. Some young women also felt pressure to have an abortion from professionals such as social workers and GPs. Fran said: 'Even the doctors were giving me stuff on abortion every time I went to see them, even though I said I wasn't having one, they couldn't get it into their heads that I didn't want an abortion.'

A number of professionals confirmed the perception that pressure is frequently put on looked after young women to have a termination. One Sure Start Plus adviser, working with teenage parents, commented:

> You often hear this from young people, that they often feel the grownups think it would be better if they have a termination, because they think they are too young, it's not the right time, the sensible thing would be to have a termination.

A specialist nurse for looked after children described the professional panic that she had observed when a young woman in care was suspected of being pregnant:

> I think if someone is suspected of being pregnant, fear sets in… Real fear and the view that at all costs it is important that this person has the pregnancy terminated. My experience in the homes is that what the staff want…even if they talk about choice, it is their fear that the person will

continue with the pregnancy. As a consequence it definitely colours the process and they want to get them off to the clinic or doctor and get the termination sorted out. Then the young person will dig their heels in.

This view was shared by a head of children's services, who reflected on the importance of balancing the timeliness of the decision to terminate a pregnancy and not placing undue pressure on a young person:

> The worst thing you can do is put the young person under pressure. If they feel you are pressurising them into making a decision and they feel they are being pushed into something, they will be very resentful and you just won't get a positive outcome, they won't listen to you, or worse, you will never see them again. Late terminations need to be avoided wherever possible, so it is a real challenge to not rush the young women into a decision, but at the same time making them aware of the milestones around termination.

Part of the need for self-sufficiency for some of the young people appeared to be linked, however, to a sense of not caring what others thought, or resisting pressure from others to tell them what to do. As Georgia explained: 'The managers [of the supported accommodation unit] gave me a lecture as usual, they said I should have an abortion. They also told me about fostering and adoption, but I just laughed at them.'

And as Mandy said when others reacted negatively to the news of her pregnancy: 'It didn't make us feel anything, I was still gonna keep it [the baby]...doesn't matter what anyone says, it's my business.'

For the young men in the study, few had been involved in the process of reaching a decision about what their girlfriend would do when pregnant. Many said they would support their girlfriend in whatever she decided. Steve, aged 20 with a one-year-old son, commented:

> We never really talked about it. I asked my girlfriend what she wanted to do about the pregnancy and she said she didn't want to get rid of it, so really it's just dealing with it 'cos I would stand by her whatever.

Peter, aged 19 and whose partner was pregnant at the time of the study, was determined to stand by his girlfriend, despite his reservations about it being the best decision for himself:

> I asked my girlfriend what she wanted to do about the pregnancy and she said she wanted to keep the baby so we just dealt with it. I said I would stand by her. She didn't like the idea of abortion. I think at first I would have

preferred to have gotten rid of it as I felt I would be tied down so young
…but now it's OK.

In many cases, however, young men either agreed with the decision made by their partner about the pregnancy, or had no say at all in whether or not a partner or ex-partner continued with a pregnancy.

ATTITUDES TO ABORTION

The majority of young women and young men interviewed held strong views against abortion and consequently did not think that they would consider any option other than continuing with the pregnancy. As Janet explained:

> I didn't believe in abortion so I knew I'd just deal with it. It's like killing another person. One of my friends had one when she was only 12 – I can understand that but I wouldn't have done it. I told my partner that if I was pregnant I wouldn't abort it and he said he wouldn't think about that anyway.

Georgia explained that her views about abortion were so strong that she could ignore the pressures from those around her to terminate the pregnancy:

> Considering the options wasn't confusing as I don't believe in abortion. I decided about three days later I would keep it. Everyone apart from my boyfriend and aunt wanted me to have an abortion, but once my mind is made up no one can change it.

Anna, 18 years old and with a 10-month-old son, spoke at length about her views about abortion:

> Everyone else suggested I have an abortion. All my friends said, 'Get rid of it, it will ruin your life, you won't be able to go out'. I couldn't…knowing that I had done something like that is disgusting, even thinking about it is awful for me… I couldn't do it… I think I would probably kill myself after I had done it…'cos I wouldn't be able to face the guilt.

Another young woman, Catherine, aged 18 when she had her first baby, had felt strongly that she should not terminate her pregnancy, especially as her decision about the pregnancy coincided with the violent death of her cousin:

> My family spoke to me about having an abortion and that and I went and got the papers but I knew that I wouldn't do it, because my cousin died, he was shot. And I thought one life gone, why am I going to end another like that?

The majority of the young men who spoke with us had similarly strong views about abortion. Ian, who was 17 and expecting a baby with his girlfriend when we spoke to him, said:

> At first I asked my girlfriend what she wanted and she said, 'I'm keeping it' and I thought 'great'. I would have supported her whatever she wanted but if she wanted an abortion we wouldn't be together now as 'it's a life' and I see it as murdering somebody.

Another significant reason given for not considering an abortion was that young people felt they needed to take 'responsibility' for having sex without using contraception. Claire, who was 20 and had two children, said:

> I don't believe in abortions, but also the way I see it – if I was old enough to fall pregnant, then I was also old enough to cope with having a child afterwards…if I am old enough to make a baby, then I am old enough to keep it. I was an adult, so I was old enough to have sex in the first place, to fall pregnant.

The only exception to these anti-abortion views was found in the London site, where half of the young women reported having considered a termination, and where one young woman had terminated a second pregnancy which occurred soon after the birth of her first child.

ATTITUDES TO ADOPTION

Young people's views of adoption were very similar to those they expressed against abortion. They associated being in care with rejection and abandonment and these experiences appeared to be the main reasons why they were against adoption. Julia, who was pregnant with her first child at 16, commented: 'I wouldn't adopt or get it fostered. As I've been fostered I know what it's like.'

As Steve, age 20 with a one-year-old son, put it:

I wouldn't put a child in care. I wouldn't have let that happen, as I've been there myself and know exactly what it's like. It was a case of keep it or get rid of it 'cos there was no way it was going into care.

Sophie said she did consider adoption or foster care when her housing situation was in crisis but commented:

I don't think adoption was ever in my head, but maybe foster care – just, you know, let me get myself together, OK, I know I am having this baby, I should have thought about this before the baby, but now I am thinking, all right just give me a year, a year to get my life on track, and then I'll get the baby back.

Katie felt she could not deal with the emotional side of having her baby adopted:

During the pregnancy I sometimes thought about adoption, but when he come out, I thought nooo; no, when you are pregnant, you feel the movement, you fall in love with it; I don't know how people can hand them over.

One of the most striking findings to emerge from our interviews with young people and professionals was the frequency with which emotional influences, such as the need to love someone, were mentioned. Although some professionals cast doubt on the need to give and receive unconditional love as a reason why young women in and from care become pregnant at a young age, a majority of the young women interviewed spoke in these terms, even if they did not often use the phrase 'unconditional love'. Young women spoke frequently about their need to love and care for someone as being reasons for wanting to continue with the pregnancy. Fran said: 'When I found out I was pregnant I was laughing and crying. I just thought I want to keep it. It will give me something to love.'

Susie, who was 17 at the time of the study and had a 10-week-old son, described some of her feelings at the time when she was faced with being pregnant: 'If I've got a baby then I know that we'll be really close. I just wanted someone to be really close with and that I can rely on him and he can rely on me.'

Karen, who was 16 when we met her and had her baby aged 15, talked, like some other young people, about the link she saw between having a baby and being in care: 'I've seen children in care actually deliberately go out and have babies 'cos it gives them a sense of some-thing to be proud of… Or you're worth something or someone to care about…like unconditionally.'

Feeling alone, the instability that results from frequent moves within the care system, along with missing the sense of being part of a family, were all mentioned and often directly linked to the desire to be a mother. Rebecca had rationalised that 'having a baby I knew would mean I wouldn't need to be hurt any more'. And, in talking about her own desire to have a baby, Sonia said: 'I was lonely. I was fed up of moving around all the time. I just wanted to be loved by someone. At that stage I wasn't close to me mum, I didn't really have my sister.'

This point was reiterated by one foster carer who had worked with many looked after young people:

> They think they're not loved… Most of them don't have parents and they want to have somebody around them, someone to love. They want to have a family and think that the only way is to go out and have a baby. Some of the kids in care are really lonely.

Some young men we spoke with tended to view the prospect of parent-hood as a chance to establish their own family. When he was 16 years old, Sean's girlfriend was pregnant with his first child. By the age of 24 when we spoke to him, Sean had gone on to have two further children. When asked about his reaction to the first pregnancy, he explained:

> I was happy about it as I don't have any background family myself. I've never met my mum or dad, and apparently I have younger brothers and sisters but never met them so I could relate to the baby as being my blood.

Other terms commonly used by both young people and professionals, in relation to having a baby, included security, purpose, focus and identity. Tanya said:

> With my first child, it's like having someone of your own to love as I'd never had that, and especially if you've been on your own a lot like me. I think that's why I was so over the moon when I got pregnant. It's almost like you have given yourself a purpose, some security… I think that's why people in homes may have them.

For some young people, having a baby was seen as providing a sense of achievement and control. Colleen summed this up:

> Even if I don't do anything else in my life, I've got this one thing that I'm gonna have for the rest of my life and I brought it into the world. I could stay on the dole for the rest of my life but I've still got something that I've done.

Sian, aged 18 with one child, saw the pregnancy as an opportunity to assert her own views and make her own decisions:

> My mum just told me to have an abortion… I was told not to have him. I decided to keep him in the end… I had always done what everyone else wanted but decided that this time I was going to do what I wanted.

Professionals we spoke with varied in their opinions concerning the extent to which young people from care viewed pregnancy and the prospect of having a child as a means of making up for the lack of emotional support they had received as children and young people. One residential social worker commented: 'I think sometimes they think the answer to their troubles or problems is to have a child…creating families of their own, families that they're never had. Seeing it as being able to control part of their life.'

However, a Sure Start Plus adviser cautioned against making assumptions about young people in care 'replacing what they never had', and also viewing their circumstances negatively:

> I don't subscribe to any one view about why anyone gets pregnant… I think they're very different individuals in very different situations and it [pregnancy] can have any multitude of meanings. It's nearly always said about young people in care that they've done it because they are emotionally deprived… I hear that a lot from professionals before they've even met the person. My view is that maybe they are and maybe they're not… It's sad that it's a sign of pathology and, therefore, it's a bad thing.

CONCLUSIONS

In this chapter we have highlighted how the young people in the study reacted to the news that they or their partner were pregnant. We have seen that, despite the initial shock that most of the young people felt, continuing with the pregnancy and becoming a mother or father was, they believed, either the best option for them at the time, or, as in the case of young men, what their partners wanted. The overwhelming majority of young people felt positively about the decision that they made and, in later chapters, we explore further some of their subsequent experiences of being a parent.

The reactions of young people, their partners and the significant adults in their lives to the discovery that they were pregnant may not be untypical in any situation where a young person becomes pregnant at an age which is socially defined as being too young. Similarly, some of the negative views and responses to the idea of abortion are not uncommon and, as we saw in Chapter 1, in most cases are likely to be influenced by broader social, class and cultural factors. That said, at least a few of the young people in the study dismissed abortion and adoption as options because they knew that these had been alternatives considered for themselves by their own parents, considerations that had left them feeling rejected and unwanted as a result.

The number of young people who were quick to dismiss abortion or adoption as realistic options was striking. The direct association that many made between these options and the rejection and abandonment that they themselves had felt as children was even more so. By acknowledging this fact, we by no means dispute the view of some professionals that young people's decisions were highly individual and were made in response to the unique circumstances of their lives at the point when they discovered that they or their partner were pregnant. On the contrary, as we will see in later chapters, not only were all of the young people who spoke with us facing extremely different situations when they made these decisions, but also they had to take into account a distinct combination of factors that were likely to either help them or create difficulties for them. What we wish to emphasise, however, is that the number of young people that attributed their decision to become a parent as an opportunity to experience love and affection was so common that it is difficult to overlook.

It is this point that brings us to one of the recurrent themes of this book, that current policies and strategies designed to prevent early pregnancy do not take into account the complex emotional factors influencing the very rational decisions that some young people make to have children when they do. As we saw in Chapter 4, contraceptive use among the young people in our study was sporadic, to say the least. Furthermore, young people rarely had access to meaningful guidance and education about relationships and sex. Yet, the fundamental reasons that many of the young people gave for choosing to go on to become parents ran far deeper than these. As such, while improving access to contraceptive services and continuing to be innovative in how we provide appropriate education and support to young people with respect to sex and relationships are laudable, they are unlikely to substantially change the likelihood that some young people who have faced adversity and upheaval will become parents in their teenage years.

We will revisit this and similar themes in later chapters. What the findings in this chapter highlight, however, are at least two implications for policy and practice that require greater attention in programme planning and intervention. First, that many young women in the study lacked access to non-directive – that is disinterested – advice about the options available to them when they discovered that they were pregnant. Second, young men more often than not, accepted their partner's choice as to whether or not to become a parent. Greater attention needs to be given, therefore, to providing independent advice and support to both young men and women faced with making decisions about a pregnancy.

Furthermore such support should come from professionals who are aware of and sensitive to young people's earlier life experiences and how these might influence their decisions about parenthood.

CHAPTER 6

BEING PREGNANT

It will bring more joy to my life,
but I know it's going to be hard.

INTRODUCTION

In this chapter we outline what young people felt and thought about pregnancy. When they spoke with us, some young women were pregnant, while others spoke about an earlier pregnancy or, if they had more than one child, compared one pregnancy with another. For the young men, some were currently with their girlfriend who was pregnant, while others talked about past relationships. All the young people highlighted the many changes that had come about as a result of the pregnancy.

Young people told us about their hopes and expectations of becoming a parent as well as their experiences of care and support during pregnancy. They spoke about the range of professionals that was involved in providing antenatal care, the social workers who, among other things, carried out pre-birth assessments, their need for somewhere suitable to live, access to education, their relationships with partners, family members, carers and friends and some of their experiences with alcohol and other drugs.

FEELINGS ABOUT PREGNANCY
AND THE PROSPECT OF PARENTHOOD

For many young people, pregnancy brought with it hopes and aspirations for future parenthood. Young people often described feeling different about themselves – and developing a different sense of responsibility, particularly regarding the need to think about caring about themselves as well as for their child. Tanya talked about the changes she had seen in herself, changes which she was certain were for the better:

> During pregnancy you feel different within yourself – like feel…become more sensible. I think I have changed a lot since I have become a mum, whereas when I was younger, I think I was a bit silly in meself; I feel differently.

For Sophie, pregnancy, she felt, motivated her in ways she had never experienced before:

> I didn't give a fuck, I didn't need to get a job, get housing, because everything I am doing just affected me, no one else. I think a baby is a way to better myself. Now I have to get a job, get myself sorted out. Now I am thinking in three years' time, I need to have a steady job, I need to have this, I need to have that and the only reason is because of this baby.

For many, pregnancy was a time of excitement about the imminent birth of their child mixed with understandable anxieties, frequently related to the ability to fulfil their role as parents and live up to the expectations and responsibilities facing them. Ian, aged 17 at the time of the study and expecting his first child with his partner, was worried about being able to cope financially:

> I'm worried as I'm not working. I only get £40 a week and I'm in debt. I feel as though I want to forget about my debt and get on with how I'm going to be able to look after the baby.

Yet Toby, aged 18 and also about to become a dad for the first time, while not expecting being a parent to be easy, felt that too much emphasis was placed on the negative aspects of having children young. He commented:

> I don't expect it to be easy and people, as we're young, do keep telling us how hard it's going to be. But I feel that they make it out to be more

negative than it is. Sometimes we feel patronised even by family members – generally older people.

Peter, aged 19, similarly shared a measured view of the prospect of becoming a father: 'It will bring more joy to my life but I know it's going to be hard.'

Quite a number of young people mentioned in passing that other family members – usually sisters, brothers or cousins – had become parents at a young age or were pregnant around the same time. These experiences made the prospect of becoming a parent rather less daunting for them and often meant they could derive a degree of support from others. When we asked Liz, who was 16 and pregnant with her first child, how she felt about becoming a single parent, since she was no longer with her partner, Liz commented: 'My sister done it so…and my mum and everyone is always there for me.'

Debbie, who had just turned 17 and was due to give birth to her baby the day after she took part in the study, commented that she did not think that having a baby at her age would mean that she missed out on opportunities. She said: 'I've done all the fun stuff I need to do… I don't need that any more.' When asked what she was looking forward to, she replied: 'Nothing specific, lots of little things – just being able to teach them… I have so many expectations about how I'm going to teach them.'

ANTENATAL CARE

Whether or not young people attended antenatal classes, and their experiences of them, appeared to depend on a number of factors – their knowledge about classes and what others said about them, the practicalities of getting there and whether they had someone to go with. A large number of young people reported not attending any antenatal classes at all. Janet, when asked whether she had attended any, replied: 'I've thought about it but don't really see the point in them and my mum said they are a waste of time.'

Kate had not attended any classes at all throughout her pregnancy as she said she 'could not face' going on her own. Adejoke, even though she did attend all her antenatal classes, would have liked to go with her boyfriend but, she said, 'he wasn't around'.

Going with someone else also helped allay young people's concerns about being judged or 'looked down on'. Jane commented:

> I was embarrassed at first as I felt I would be judged as I look young for my age and also because I wasn't married. It was better when a friend came with me and once I got to know people it was OK.

Although Sophie had attended one or two antenatal sessions, she stopped going because, 'I felt a bit naive because she [midwife] would say something and I would be like "What are you on about again?" And everyone would look at me as if to say, "Don't you know that?"'.

Martha also commented on the generally negative attitudes others held about her. She disliked, she said, the way the midwives had treated her and the attitudes they appeared to hold about her due to her experiences of being in care. 'It was their attitude...they kept telling me what to do and they brought up the fact that I had been in care. It was like they were making assumptions about the kind of mother I would be.'

Toby and his partner also felt that they were being judged because of their background – this time by a GP. They found the GP somewhat unhelpful and dismissive of their anxieties and concerns in the early stages of pregnancy. Toby said:

> If you're a teenage parent doctors don't really care! They think 'another no hoper'. A lot of young people get put off going to doctors as they don't make eye contact with you and don't offer much support – I think they treat us this way as we're young and you can feel awkward. Our doctor just didn't seem to care.

Jane, who was pregnant with her first child at 17, said of her GP: 'I felt that he was looking down on me when I said I was pregnant.'

As often as reporting negative experiences of services during pregnancy, however, young people spoke positively about the antenatal care they had received. Many young people who did so highlighted the role of personalised or specialist provision – such as one-to-one support or specialist teenage pregnancy midwives.

Compared with antenatal classes, direct, one-to-one support provided by a midwife through antenatal appointments was more often spoken of positively and young people said they would be more likely to attend these appointments. Janet had resisted attending antenatal group sessions, but described how she had benefited from the individual support of her midwife: 'She's been helpful as I've been paranoid…every little move the baby makes I get worried.'

Specialist teenage pregnancy midwives, appointed through programmes such as Sure Start Plus (which existed at the time in two of the four research sites) or other specialist teenage midwifery services, were particularly valued by young people. Michelle commented: 'I had a good midwife…a really good midwife…she was really nice… I started seeing her when I was 14 weeks pregnant and she supports me even now… I drop in to see her.'

Liz also commented about how her specialist teenage pregnancy midwife not only provided maternity care but also helped to liaise between the different agencies she came into contact with and provided a flexible service: 'She is very good and makes contact with the social workers, and gives me home visits when I haven't got the energy to get up.'

Sarah, who had a drug problem throughout her second pregnancy, described how her specialist drugs liaison midwife was helpful: 'She knew how to deal with the situation and understood the issue. She didn't just tell me to stop [taking drugs] but she was able to look at your psychological well-being as well.'

Adejoke, who had had her two-year-old daughter when she was 16 years old, described how her midwife had put her in touch with a scheme, through which she was given a 'befriender' throughout her pregnancy:

> When I was pregnant, I got a friend. I'm really close with her now – she's my daughter's godmother. But she doesn't work with them [organisation] no more, but we're still friends. She was there when I was having the baby and everything.

Although personalised and specialist provision was often talked of positively by young people, they also indicated that it was not specialist provision per se that they valued, but the characteristics of the relationship a professional was able to develop with them. Some midwives, for example, were said to be understanding, caring and non-judgemental and as a result young people felt able to talk with them. Among health visitors, the approach and attitudes valued were similarly empathy, being non-judgemental, and being willing to listen and to give them time.

Amy, who had her first child at the age of 15, and who was 18 at the time of the study, said of her health visitor: 'She came around every day to see how I was doing when I was in care, and they were lovely, they asked how I was coping'.

Despite Mandy's reservations on first meeting her health visitor, over time she was able to get to know her and build a rapport with her. She explained:

> I didn't like her at first because I thought she was a bit of a snobby person...
> But once I got know her more, I think she's lovely... She sits and listens
> to us, even if it's not about the baby, but I need to talk, she sits and will listen
> to us.

Susie found her GP to be very supportive, particularly when compared with the family planning centre where, she said, staff had not been at all helpful when she discovered that she was pregnant:

> The way he talks to you was good. At the clinic [family planning centre]
> where I went for the pregnancy test, all the lady was going on about was
> that I should get rid of the baby. I should have complained about it, I think
> she was saying it because I'm Black.

Although Ian had been anxious about supporting his partner and the baby, he talked of how he found the antenatal advice and support helpful:

> Going to the scans has been really exciting and I'm going to all her appoint-
> ments and to the classes. The pregnancy kits given by the doctor and
> midwife are helpful. I am learning a lot from these about what is happening
> to her body and the baby's growth and about becoming a dad.

Young people also reported there to be a lack of consistency regarding who provided antenatal care. Many young people described mixed experiences of such care. On occasions, a new professional was reported to be better than the last. However, more often than not, young people commented unfavourably about being moved from a professional they liked to one they did not.

Karen, who was 16 when she had her first child, described the invaluable support that her specialist midwife gave her throughout the time when her daughter was placed (before she was born) on the child protection register:

> I loved my midwife, she was lovely. I sent her a card and a picture when my daughter was born. She used to come to all the child protection confer-ences and everything and she was really good, she was brilliant. She knew my background from when I was born and what's happened to me and what was going to happen with my daughter. Then they just decided that I needed to be transferred [to another midwife].

Lucy commented on how she really liked her health visitor but unfortu-nately was not able to continue seeing her: 'She [health visitor] was lovely, she didn't judge me. But I only saw her three times and had to move so I changed health visitor.'

A new placement or change in accommodation could mean that, even when young people had a GP that they liked or had got to know, they had to register again at a new practice. Debbie had had to move during her pregnancy from her previous GP, who she liked and thought had been 'very helpful', to one who she did not like. On occasion, a young person's move from one area to another was managed in such a way that young people could stay with the same GP. Despite all the upheaval that Emma had known in her life, for example, she had been able to stay registered with the same GP practice for five years: 'He [GP] has always given the right advice. …they're really lovely people…their personalities are nice as well… I just love them. They're like an exten-sion of my family if you like'..

SOCIAL SERVICES

Pre-birth assessments were a cause of great anxiety for many young people, as were subsequent assessments after their babies were born. Lucy, for example, described how from the time when she was eight weeks pregnant and throughout the pregnancy, she was 'assessed', a process she found to be particularly stressful:

> They asked lots of questions and observed [me] all the time. I felt stressed at the time and kept taking it out on everybody. If someone was doing something to themselves then OK to protect the child but I wasn't doing

anything wrong but they went on past history – my mum was on the smack
and they thought I might do it.

When we spoke with her, Julia said that her social worker was preparing
her for a pre-birth assessment. She described how, every Friday, she and
her boyfriend had to go to the family centre to participate in sessions
which she mostly found unhelpful. She commented: 'They cover stuff I
already know but I go to get through the assessment. It annoys me that I
have to prove that I am going to be a good parent.'

Mary resented being under close scrutiny when, at 16 years old, she
was pregnant with the first of her two children. She said of social
services:

They interfered a lot when I was pregnant. They were nosy and wanted to
know who the father was. The hospital social worker told social services I
was pregnant and how far gone I was so they could work out if I had sex
before 16.

Toby talked of how his earlier experiences of social services as a child
affected how he felt about contacting social services for support. He
remembered a childhood in which social workers would always be
visiting and he felt that everyone knew his business. Yet, 'when you had a
problem, you didn't always know who to call. I had so many social
workers and so many changes…it really puts you off getting help'.

Debbie, who was about to give birth to her first child, described how
her social worker was not helpful as they had tried to send her to a
mother and baby unit outside of the city where she was living. She really
did not want to go and felt that her social worker was not listening to her.
At this point, Debbie was living in temporary accommodation with her
partner and they were planning to marry soon after the arrival of the
baby. The unit they were about to send her to would not allow her
partner to stay. Debbie commented: 'There is a big sign on the wall
saying "no men allowed"'. She preferred to stay in the accommodation
where she was with her partner, although reflected that she would not
have liked to stay there once the baby was born. In particular, she had
been very distressed at witnessing another pregnant young woman being
repeatedly beaten by her partner but was unable to do anything about it.
Despite the frustrations with her social worker, however, Debbie

reflected: 'I don't blame her... she is a very nice person but she has so many rules and regulations to stick to.'

Yet, while many young people described the anxieties of what they perceived as being 'checked up on' by social services, others appeared to appreciate the additional support that was provided. Mandy said that, although she was determined to have a healthy pregnancy, she also felt that she needed the help and supervision of the residential social workers to help her achieve this, even though this entailed a high degree of supervision and surveillance: 'They gave us more help actually, like going for shopping, giving a hand, made sure I didn't do things I used to do before...so they kept a close eye on us.'

Similarly, Liz had been given an ultimatum by her social worker to either finish with her partner, who was violent, or face having her baby removed at birth. On the whole she felt that she had coped well with the break-up with her boyfriend and had been given a lot of support.

Young people frequently contrasted the type of support they received from specialist leaving care workers compared with that from more generalist social workers. Leaving care workers were described as having more regular contact with young people, offering them practical and emotional support and as having a different approach to working with them, typified as being less judgemental, more honest, more supportive and having more time to spend with young people than their regular social workers. Jane described the ongoing and regular support she received throughout her pregnancy from an assistant leaving care worker: 'During the pregnancy she visited once and sometimes twice a week, she told me about options available to me when I was pregnant like antenatal classes. She talked about her own pregnancy and about post-natal depression.'

Liz drew a striking contrast between how she perceived her leaving care social worker compared with other social workers she had worked with in the past:

> She's honest, unlike other social workers who say something to you and then go back to them [social services] and say something else. She's always said either him [partner] or the baby. She is always at the end of the phone and, on my down days, she rings me, and talks me through it...she's really

helped with my mum and that just in case something starts going wrong. That's what me and my mum need, making us talk.

Toby, however, described how he got frustrated with the lack of support provided through the leaving care service, although at the time of the study he did acknowledge that his current worker was trying hard to sort out his leaving care grant. This said, he resented the intrusive and insulting nature of the support he received when he asked about help with accommodation to take account of the fact that he had a partner and was about to become a parent. He said: 'They asked questions about my mental health and whether I was sure the baby was mine. They asked a lot of questions about my partner's family too. I think it can be too much hassle.'

For those young women in residential homes or foster care at the time of their pregnancies, their perceptions of the quality of the support they received appeared to be influenced more by the type of relationship that they developed with a carer, than by the type of placement.

Emma, though 21 at the time of the study, had been just 15 years old and in foster care when she was pregnant with her first child. Emma felt that her particular foster placement had not been the best place for her since her foster mother did not really have the right skills and knowledge to support her. She commented:

As a first mother so young, I needed a lot more advice than I did have and I shouldn't have been in a foster care placement 'cos she didn't have a clue…she was just a bit confusing… I should have been taken to a young mum's place… I should have been encouraged to go to a young mum's group – but I was influenced by my ex-partner and his family which didn't help.

Amy, who was 15 at the time of her pregnancy, said of the staff in her residential care home:

I stayed there for about eight months with the baby. They were kind and loving and never once was I left to be sick on my own and they said it was all right to talk to them whenever I needed it…they were lovely.

HOUSING

In all four research sites – in the north of England, central England, London and southern England – young people talked about their difficulties in accessing adequate, appropriate and affordable housing during their pregnancies. Young people and professionals, alike, noted the importance of access to accommodation. Since becoming pregnant, Julia had experienced a series of foster placements in quick succession and stressed the significance of having somewhere permanent to live before having her baby: 'It's important for me to have a flat, to be prepared for my baby, to have my own place so that I can prove to people what I can do…to be settled, when I've moved around so much.'

The central importance of housing was summed up by one social worker: 'Without housing, everything suffers. They can't focus on anything else if they have nowhere to live.'

At the time of interview, most young people we spoke with were in some form of temporary or uncertain housing situation. This was either a foster or residential care placement that was likely to finish within the near future or at a stage in the local council housing allocation process which meant that a further change in accommodation was inevitable. Liz, for example, hoped to secure a place in a mother and baby unit where she would have access to supported accommodation. She spoke of how her sister had been to stay there before she had her baby and 'did really well' and her cousin was at the time of the study resident in the unit. Yet, despite their hopes, young people found suitable accommodation hard to come by.

When Toby and his partner first learned about their pregnancy, they were in private accommodation where children were not allowed to stay. They therefore went to the local council to ask for accommodation and were told that they would have to make themselves homeless first. As a result they were placed in temporary accommodation which, as Toby explains, had its drawbacks:

> We were put in a B&B [bed and breakfast accommodation] for two months on the top floor and, although we were lucky to get this, there are some dodgy characters like drug addicts staying in these places as we experienced. We were allowed to stay in during the day as we were both working night shifts.

Toby went on to say that the support he was offered through the leaving care services was unhelpful and failed to take account of his new family status:

> When we found out my partner was pregnant, I was offered help but not her or the baby. I was offered a one bedroom flat and told she could sleep at the flat but not live there as she was not a care leaver – this made me feel like I was 10 again. I decided to sort things out myself.

Given the lack of appropriate accommodation available to many young people, a risk reduction approach was, according to professionals, often adopted. One leaving care worker explained:

> We have to take all kinds of risks and [even] place young people in situations where they may be at risk of exploitation. But I have a no nonsense approach and tell young people if there is a concern. You do your best, check out the landlord and accommodation. But at the end of the day, the young person is either homeless or they live there.

Uncertainty regarding the security of the accommodation could be stressful for young people – and possibly dangerous, not only for pregnant young women but also for any existing children. For Emma, the uncertainty of her housing situation while she was pregnant created a great deal of additional stress for her:

> Finding places to stay with social services is really difficult and I had a lot of problems with that at first. I was lucky that I had my boyfriend that I could have somewhere to stay if nothing was working. It's not just pregnant people but young people anyway who have this problem, but especially pregnant people they should have somewhere found on the dot. Because I was getting all sorts of ideas about what I was going to do…or should I just try and kill myself, I wanted to keep it [the baby] but I was thinking I was going to be pregnant and homeless, I had all sorts of thoughts.

Finding herself homeless when pregnant with her second child, Emma was given no advice about what she should do. She said that she did not go to stay in hostels but, instead, 'stayed with men who were attracted to me and I was to them'.

For some young pregnant women, being reliant on the accommodation provided by partners generated a lot of insecurity. Sophie, aged 17, seven months pregnant and living unofficially in her boyfriend's shared house, said:

> If we have an argument, which happens quite often, he can tell me to get out… It's the baby that he wants… I don't think I'd be here unless it was for the baby. So, I am worried that he is going to get this place to live, and say to social services department, '[she] hasn't got anywhere to live, I'll have the baby'. I don't think he will, because he is a nice guy, but there is always a chance.

A leaving care social worker described a similar situation with a young woman who she was working with, who was soon to give birth:

> She is sleeping on the floor, staying with her boyfriend… She would finish with him but she has nowhere to live… She is at risk. So, she is a care leaver, and homeless, so the child will be on the register. He has gone off with someone else, but she had to have him back to have somewhere to live. As a woman and pregnant, she shouldn't have to forgive him and sleep with him again. [Effectively], they are both forced into a situation that isn't natural.

Sophie went on to say that, because she had been deemed intentionally homeless (as she was evicted from her previous house), her only immediate option other than private renting, which she could not afford, was to go to a homeless shelter. She commented:

> My baby is due in three months, so how am I going to live in a single person's night shelter? They [social services] have said that if I am still living there when the baby is born that it will be taken off me. Is that their answer to that?

Sophie was clearly bemused by the fact that although she was willing to go into a mother and baby unit – even though her partner could not stay with her – because of her earlier eviction, she first had to rent somewhere privately for six months before she could enter the unit. She said:

> I can't understand how that is possible when the baby is due in three months. I will do anything to make sure my child is not taken into care and I can't believe that the cost of taking the baby is less than helping me live somewhere with the baby.

Sophie was not the only young woman who found she was chiefly by herself when it came to navigating the complexities of bureaucratic housing systems. However, Debbie and Catherine had been helped and they found such assistance invaluable in finding somewhere to live. Debbie, who was nine months pregnant with her first child, described how it was her youth offending team worker who had assisted her in accessing housing even though it was not necessarily her remit to do so:

> She came to the housing offices with me, she rang up places for me, rang up the district council for me. She just generally let me talk to her really, because I was getting so worked up about it. Everyone was saying to me, 'No you can't do this you have to go to the mother and baby unit'.

Catherine was 18 when she was pregnant with her son and not sure what to do. She described the invaluable support she had received from the manager of a single mothers' hostel, who helped her to access next stage housing:

> I decided I was going to keep the baby and then things picked up. I got a job, I moved out of that hostel, I moved to [a specialist unit for pregnant young women] and started college. If it wasn't for the manager of the hostel, I wouldn't be here today.

EDUCATION

Few of the young people we spoke to were attending school or accessing alternative educational provision at the time of their pregnancy. For those who were, the response of schools and other services was again mixed. While Sally, who was aged 16 at the time, had wanted to stay on at school and sit her GCSE exams, her head of year had decided that she could not do so because of 'health and safety' reasons. In fact, this decision was contrary to government guidance at the time that emphasised the importance of enabling young pregnant women to remain in school throughout their pregnancies. Bridget, who was 15 when she was pregnant, felt that the home tutor she had straight after giving birth to her son was insensitive and 'would get annoyed if I wanted to go and see to the baby'.

Julia talked of the invaluable support she had from a Sure Start adviser who she met when she was three months pregnant and still attending school. Both the midwife and the adviser visited the school to help sort out the best support strategy for her which, Julia felt, had helped alleviate the stress she was feeling. In addition the school counsellor, 'a lovely lady', had been one of the first people who Julia had trusted to tell about the pregnancy: 'I knew she would say nothing.' As a result of this support and despite mixed reactions from teachers, some of whom 'made rude comments, gave me dirty looks, treated me like a bit of dirt', Julia had stayed on at school and had just finished Year 10 at the time of the research. Emma, a few years earlier, had been aged 15 when pregnant with her first child and she was placed in a specialist unit for pregnant pupils. She commented:

> It wasn't a proper school, the teachers weren't trying, the work wasn't proper school work – and then I was six months pregnant so I left. Now, I'd love to go and do a few college courses, I'd like to do childcare and drama – I'm interested in drama and that.

PARTNERS, FAMILY, CARERS AND FRIENDS

Many of the young women we spoke with felt that their relationships with the fathers of their babies were going well. A significant minority, however, were in more challenging or unsupportive relationships.

Julia described how she was enjoying being pregnant and the prospect of becoming a parent. She felt that her relationship with her boyfriend (also 17 years old) had improved since the pregnancy and commented: 'We have built our relationship around the pregnancy and it has got better – he tells me that he will stay with me.'

Mandy, on the other hand, who was aged 17 when we spoke with her and had a three-month-old daughter, described how the relationship with the baby's father finished just three weeks after she discovered she was pregnant. Although her ex-partner did try to reconcile the relationship a few months later, Mandy decided that this was not the best thing for her and her child since he tended to drink alcohol excessively and rarely offered much in the way of financial support to bring up their daughter. Similarly, Claire, who was aged 19 and with a two-year-old son, split up with her partner when she was four months pregnant. Catherine, who was 20 years old when we spoke with her, said that when aged 17 she had been living in a hostel and pregnant and stated that at the time her partner 'just did not want to know'.

A few young women dealt with domestic violence during their pregnancies. Liz described an incident when her boyfriend tried to strangle her and, although she felt confident about the support she would receive from her mother and sister after the birth of her baby, she still had some anxieties that her ex-partner would become involved. He had threatened to take the baby away from her once it was born and Liz described how, with the help of her social worker and her mother, she planned to take out a court injunction against him.

For young men, their personal circumstances and the relationship with girlfriends or ex-girlfriends often left them uncertain as to what role they might best take during pregnancy or when the baby was born. David was in custody in a youth offender institution at the time when we spoke with him. He had been shocked when his ex-girlfriend announced that she was expecting a child since he had been told that, due to an earlier medical condition, she was unable to become pregnant. Although his girlfriend claimed that David was the father of the baby, he had been left unsure over whether the baby was his or was fathered by his ex-partner's new boyfriend. He stated that he felt frustrated, uninformed and powerless about the situation and did not know what role he would have in the life of the child.

Support from family members, carers and friends was said to be somewhat more dependable, although not necessarily so. Tanya, aged 18 years when she gave birth to her daughter, described how her grand-mother let her stay with her for the two weeks before she gave birth and, for the two weeks after the baby was born, she stayed with her older sister. Both her grandmother and her sister were with her when she gave birth.

It was Sally's foster parents who gave her the most support during pregnancy, even though she no longer lived with them during that period. Leticia, too, found that her (more recent) foster carers provided her with good practical and emotional help throughout her pregnancy. Her foster mother attended the birth and had encouraged Leticia to let her partner also be there.

While Julia particularly valued emotional support from her current carer, she also found it of help when her two previous foster carers assisted with practical matters such as purchasing maternity clothes or organising her money. Importantly, too, she trusted that they would not give any negative feedback to the social services department. She commented: 'My foster carers do a lot and do provide feedback to social services but what social services want to hear is very different.'

Whether or not they had support from their own parents, some young people talked of the help they had from the parents of partners who had not been in care. This type of support ranged from buying equipment or clothes for the baby, helping them get to antenatal appointments or scans, providing them with at least some temporary accommodation or helping them prepare in other ways for the arrival of the baby.

Young women frequently described friends as an important source of support, particularly those who were also pregnant or who had children. A number commented that many of their friends were also pregnant at the same time and were, as Liz said, 'settling down' after what she depicted as quite turbulent years during which they had often been 'in trouble'.

However, some young women, like Jane, found that, once pregnant, 'I felt excluded from my group of friends who were not pregnant and this was not so good'. On the whole, young men were less likely to describe friends as a source of support throughout the pregnancy. Steve commented that he hardly talked about the pregnancy with his friends at the time because 'We don't talk about things like that, we go racing cars, play football and have a laugh'.

DRUG USE

The use of drugs was often talked about by young people with regard to their experiences of pregnancy, although they usually did not make a distinction between the different types of drugs they were using. Substances they did mention using included cannabis, amphetamines, ecstasy and crack cocaine, as well as alcohol. Some young people stated that, prior to learning that they or their partner were pregnant, they used one or another or a combination of these drugs fairly regularly. For most young people who used drugs or alcohol, pregnancy was given as a reason for either modifying or ceasing their alcohol or drug use. However, some other young people described ongoing difficulties with drug use and the ways in which this affected their pregnancies and (consequently) their perceived ability to parent. Others commented that, in order to limit or cease their drug use, they had to detach themselves from important friendships with whom, and social networks within which, they used drugs regularly.

Before she was pregnant, Mandy talked about how she just saw taking drugs as a part of life. On realising she was pregnant, however, she felt she knew that she would have to stop taking drugs since 'I was responsible for someone else now, and not just myself'. Mandy described how she had to change her friendship groups once discovering that she was pregnant and moved away from those who were taking drugs.

Sarah, who was 22 years old when we spoke with her, had a daughter when she was 17 and a son when aged 19. Although she had been taking crack cocaine for a number of years at the time when she was pregnant for the first time, Sarah described how her partner at the time had forced her to stop taking drugs throughout the pregnancy. Her son, born two years later, however, was born with neonatal withdrawal and had a low birth weight.

After losing custody of her first child and while pregnant with her second, Emma was homeless and 'addicted to crack'. The violence she had experienced in her life, she said, accounted for her drug use. While living in temporary accommodation, for example, she was abducted and held against her will for two weeks, raped violently and so badly beaten that 'you couldn't even see who I was'. Emma also stated that she had been sexually abused when she was living with her adoptive parents and concluded: 'I've been through so many things… I'm not surprised that I turned to drugs.' She added: 'I met the wrong people while I was homeless. About a year after I was homeless, I ended up trying certain drugs, got addicted to crack, badly addicted in the end.'

On discovering that she was pregnant, Emma had stopped taking crack but was still homeless. She talked of how she was turned away from one hostel because she was pregnant. Throughout the pregnancy, Emma was anxious that having taken crack and other drugs in early pregnancy would have affected her daughter:

> I was very scared and didn't want to have the baby…because I was on drugs when I found out I was pregnant. I thought the baby would come out all messed up and stuff and I wouldn't have been able to handle that.

Despite her worries, Emma went on to give birth to a 'perfect' daughter several months later. Although her partner at the time wanted her to have the baby and to stay with her, Emma made an important decision at the time she decided to continue with the pregnancy: 'He [boyfriend] said "we can work it out", but he was smoking crack as well and I said to myself "Even if I do keep the baby, I'm not staying with him anyway".'

At the time of the study, two years after the birth of her daughter, Emma said that she had not seen her ex-partner at all. She had been given support from her adoptive parents to stay off of drugs. She had also married someone that she met during her pregnancy who, she said, had been happy to be a father to her daughter.

CONCLUSIONS

The young women who spoke with us faced many challenges during their pregnancies – finding the right sorts of antenatal care, resisting unwelcome scrutiny from social services, facing prejudice about being in care or being young and pregnant, trying to find adequate accommodation, accessing education, dealing with violent partners and coping with drugs. Notwithstanding those relationships that were violent and abusive, some young men too struggled to identify their roles as prospective father.

However, despite these challenges, young people were often able to name individuals – whether family members, partners, or specific professionals – who had made a real difference to their lives. They often spoke with clarity about the qualities that attracted them to, or distanced them from, the many services with which they came into contact. Being listened to by trustworthy adults, who neither judged nor patronised them, was a feature of relationships considered as important. These qualities, as we highlight in the next chapter, were also important to young people once they became parents.

CHAPTER 7

BEING A MUM, BEING A DAD

I am really proud of my son and of myself, and the way
I've brought him up, and the fact I've done it myself.

INTRODUCTION

As highlighted earlier, as young people move through, or in and out of,
the public care system, the relationships they build with others around
them have a profound effect on how they adapt and respond to the new
circumstances they encounter. In this chapter, we explore how those
young people who took part in the study talked about their lives as new
parents.

The focus here is on the meanings that both young men and young
women associated with parenthood, what they enjoyed, the challenges
they faced and from where they derived their emotional support. Under-
pinning this analysis we define the types and nature of the relationships
that young people encountered and the extent to which these helped or
hindered them in assuming their new identities and roles.

The young parents who spoke with us on the whole had a great deal
to say about becoming parents. Their experiences provoked a range of
reactions from ourselves as researchers and we were at times variably
shocked, surprised and even horrified by what we heard. There were,
however, many experiences which were striking in their ordinariness.
Young people were, on the whole, coping well as new parents – sometimes despite having faced extreme adversity.

This observation is an important one and brings us to a recurrent theme throughout this book – that, rather than limiting their opportunities, many young people we spoke to felt that early parenthood had broadened their horizons, given them new chances or positively impacted on their sense of well-being.

A TIME OF CHANGE

For several young people we spoke with, becoming a parent was described as an event which led them to rethink their lives and their priorities. When she spoke with us, Lucy had a one-year-old son. She stated that she no longer felt a desire to lead the same sort of life she had before he was born:

> Having a child has calmed me down. I used to take drugs all the time like smoking dope until I found out I was pregnant. I used to get locked up all the time but I don't any more. I stopped drinking as well as I was a right alcoholic, but I still smoked cigarettes. He [the baby] never asked to be there but he was there so I had to stop all those things.

For a number of young men, becoming a parent provided them with a new sense of responsibility. Fatherhood was, some noted, a time to rethink their lives and to strive for change. Brandon had been candid about the number of times he had been in trouble with the police. Fatherhood had, he suggested:

> made me more responsible. It has made me realise I can't get into trouble. I don't want to be in jail at 21 for five years or whatever and I get out and my baby is not a baby any more... I'd miss out.

Ben, who was in custody (in a young offenders' institution) at the time of the study, felt that he too had to change certain things in his life if he was going to be able to take care of his children:

> It didn't really change me but I was thinking that I need to get away from friends [who led him into trouble], get a job, look after the kids. My dad died when I was young so I didn't want that for my kids, I wanted to be there for them. It has changed the way I think... My daughter's going to be with me... I'll be relaxing with my daughter when I am on tag [on probation if he gets early release].

Similarly, Danny, just 15 years old and in a secure unit for burglary and 'handling stolen goods', described how he was determined not to return to custody again but instead wanted to 'set up home':

> When I get out I'm not going to come back inside… I am just going to stay with my missus. I've missed the good parts of his [baby's life]… He's just starting to talk… He won't be saying 'Daddy' and that, he'll just be saying 'Mum'. When I get out I'm just going to spend as much time with him as I can.

Many professionals recognised, too, that there may be potential benefits for some young people in care in becoming parents at a young age, particularly where their own childhoods had been less than straightforward. One teenage pregnancy coordinator commented:

> Some young people choose to have babies for very positive reasons and I think it's important we don't lose sight of that as for some young people it's a defining and positive moment for them. For some young women, in particular, they do not feel that they are forfeiting anything in terms of life choices.

NEW RESPONSIBILITIES, NEW CHALLENGES

On the whole, the young people we spoke with generally looked forward to becoming parents. However, they also stated that being a parent brought with it challenges – although a number of these appeared to be no more than any new parent might face. Having their freedom curtailed, for example, was mentioned by quite a few young people. Siobhan, when asked whether there were things that were not so good about being a parent, replied:

> Not being able to do the things I should be doing at my age like going out at weekends, going down the pub at weekends with my friends. Unless I can find a babysitter I can't go out with my friends and that's the only thing really. It's not a major thing, I weren't really one for going out a lot anyway but every now and then I think, 'I really fancy going out but I can't'.

Marie had similar feelings but also described some of the challenges she faced in bringing up her son, who was almost two:

> I find it really hard…he [baby] is at a really awkward stage at the moment –
> horrible paddies…just not being able to say I am going down the pub or I
> am going to do this… I've got to find a babysitter. I am not that maternal…
> I get bored quickly when I am playing games with him. He gets bored
> quickly too and I think, 'Oh what do I do now?'

Some of the difficulties young people faced were rather more related to the testing circumstances of their lives more generally – being in custody, difficulties of developing a relationship with a partner, uncertainty about paternity and, on occasions, ongoing problems with drugs or alcohol. The young men we spoke with highlighted a number of these sorts of challenges.

Ben felt removed from the realities of being a father due to being in custody. While he said he was keen to 'be there' for his children, he mentioned that there were obstacles in the way. He indicated that he and his current girlfriend (the mother of his first daughter) needed counselling in order for them to work out their differences. He also indicated that he might not pursue gaining access to his son but clearly had mixed feelings about this: 'I don't really know enough [about how to maintain contact with his son] but I don't want to put the mum under any stress. I just want to be with my son.'

Other young men we spoke with, and who were already fathers, described complicated relationships that made it more difficult to be engaged as fully as they would wish in their children's lives. David, aged 18 at the time of research (and 17 years old when his ex-partner's daughter was born), described his confusion and anger about the situation with his ex-partner and her eight-month-old baby. His former partner now had a new boyfriend and the two of them were living together with the baby as a family.

Alex, who was 22 years old when we spoke with him, had become a father for the first time when he was aged 16. Although the pregnancy had not been planned, Alex stayed with his partner (the mother of the baby) until he was 19 years old, having a second child with her at the age of 17. Since splitting up from his ex-partner, he saw his first two children only once every two months. This was because his ex-partner had moved from the South West of England to the North West and had a new husband. Although he described feeling threatened by the new husband at first, Alex recognised that his children were happy and did not want to confuse them about who their father was. Alex felt that, although he did not regret having his children, he now believed that 'you should wait until you have a stable relationship, good job and good money…at the time you think you are grown up'.

Timothy, aged 21 when we spoke with him, had also become a father for the first time at 16 and had subsequently gone on to father two more children. He commented: 'I have a lot of heartache when I think about my other two children but can't make contact with them as I have a tricky relationship with my ex-wife and people around her.'

Sometimes, young men also reported being uncertain about the paternity of their children, a factor that led to them undergoing, or planning to undergo, a paternity test. David was in a young offenders' institution at the time of the research and, as a result, had not yet seen his daughter, who was just a few months old. He knew that his ex-girlfriend and partner were providing the baby with 'a stable family…and that's something that I've never had so it's something I want for her'. However, he still thought that he wanted to play a part in his daughter's life – if he was actually the father:

> It could be mine, it's possible. I am going for a court order and a DNA test to find out. I need to know. I need to see her [baby] to know if she's mine or not but I haven't seen her yet. Everything is bad… I can't see her [daughter]. I don't know where they live, I'm not allowed to see her, I don't know where she is. I don't know what she looks like. I don't know if she's mine.

Brandon justified his reasons for having a DNA test as follows:

> I missed it when my baby was born…because I didn't believe it was mine… So I had to say that I want a blood test because I don't want to bring up a kid until it's like 13, and then she says, 'That's not your son!'

The frustrations with bureaucracy and systems in relation to child custody were particularly evident for the young men who we interviewed. Yet these were often combined with a sense of powerlessness and inertia. Tackling the system often seemed too overwhelming a prospect – this particularly being the case when the young men had access to few financial resources. James talked of how he had a history of drug use – 'I went through a bad stage of drugs for two years' – and felt that his ex-partner was bound to bring this up should he ever make a case for custody of his son. He reflected:

> Why has the woman got all the rights [in relation to custody]? If I was finan-cially stable I would take my ex to court. Damn right I would take her to court. I have seen him [son] only a few times since she left. I was going to call in mediation but what's the point?

A number of young people spoke about taking drugs. However, many of those who were now parents stated that, despite what they had done in the past, drug use was now not a central feature of their lives. Having children, a number of young people stated, had 'calmed' them. They did not want to bring their children into environments dominated by drugs.

Moreover, a few young people commented that, if they had not become a parent, then drug use would have taken over their lives com-pletely. Indeed, for a few young people, problematic drug use was associ-ated with not being able to continue to care for a child. One professional, for example, spoke about a young woman who turned to drugs after her children had been taken into care. And Theresa described how she turned to drugs after her daughter was placed for adoption:

> At the time after losing her, I was doing drugs – pills, dope, speed. I wasn't doing it before – [only] after – I need something to take away the pain. If you lose your baby they should still be there for you…nobody was there after they took the baby.

POST-NATAL DEPRESSION

While there were some issues that men chiefly talked about, young women had their own particular concerns. Feelings of depression were frequently described by young women. Rebecca and Naomi, for example, said they often felt depressed or 'low' after having their children and felt unable to ask for help. For Katie, who was 17 years old when her son was born, being depressed following the birth of her son had led her to start to 'push him away'. She found it hard to deal with the situa-tion and ended up running away with him as she just wanted to 'escape'. She later returned home where her mother took care of her baby for a while to 'give me a break'. She then went to her GP to get help and following that 'started growing closer to him [the baby] again'.

For Amy, anxieties about what would happen if she acknowledged that she was not coping and needed help prevented her for some time from asking for support:

> I didn't tell anyone as I was scared of losing him [son]. Every time I wanted to cry I just went to my room and cried. But in the end I had to speak to someone as I thought I was going to crack.

Mandy described how she tried to hide her depression from everyone:

> It wasn't until after I had her [the baby], because it is a big difference from moving from a house full of eight people, to one by myself, I wasn't by myself when I first moved in, because my family were always around, and then I was by myself again, I couldn't cope really well, I had depression. I managed to hide it from all my family, but [my social worker] realised, she noticed one day when I was talking to one of the ladies, because I was really lonely.

VIOLENCE

For young women, in particular, experiences of violence while in care were common and continued to be so for them as mothers. Young women often described relationships where partners had on occasions been violent. At least nine of the young women in the study described violent relationships with previous partners who were the fathers of their children. Some also mentioned even earlier relationships in which they had endured such violence. Several young women described how their social workers had told them to make a choice between a partner and their child when they were known to be with a violent partner. Others fled from relationships when they realised that they were not going to improve and where they feared for the safety of their children.

Those professionals we spoke with frequently talked of the concerns that they had about young women being in violent relationships or being vulnerable to other forms of domestic violence – concerns which were heightened once they had a child. Having support to deal with issues of domestic violence, such as appropriate training or being able to refer young women to safe refuges, were highly valued by those working with young parents.

However, we also found examples of young men providing support to their partners after they had left a violent relationship. Even so, both young people and professionals stated that young men were often thought of as if not actually violent then potentially so. This, it was said, could result in young fathers being excluded from taking part in family activities and not encouraged to engage in any meaningful way with their children. Young men could be too easily viewed as a threat to, rather an asset for, the well-being of a young woman and her baby.

RELATIONSHIPS WITH PARTNERS

Of the young women we spoke with in our study, around half had a partner at the time of interview. This was usually, but not always, the father of one of their children or an expected child. A little under half of the young women stated that they did not have a current partner, and a few described their relationship with a partner as being 'on and off'. Of the young men interviewed, around half said that they were with the mother of at least one of their children, and a little under half said that they were no longer with the mother of any of their children.

Although not always the case, a number of young women described receiving sporadic, inconsistent or no support at all from their partners. Serena's partner was seven years older than her and although he did help out when her son was first born this stopped when her son was around nine months old. Mandy, who had decided not to stay with her partner (partly as a result of his drink problem), talked of her dissatisfaction at her partner's inconsistent visits to see their daughter:

> There's no real involvement. He still drinks a lot but I think he has changed a lot too. He comes to see her from time to time, he hasn't spent much money on her yet, which I am really annoyed about, he pays no mainte-nance. I am going to say that he comes on regular days to see her [daughter], not whenever it suits him because she's going to think he's just a friend, if he comes and goes, not her dad.

Amy also felt let down by her ex-partner, the father of her son:

I sent a father's day card and there was no response. I tried to keep contact. Last year we arranged to meet him in town and he never showed up. I was crying my eyes out in the town. He's even asked for a blood test to check he is the father! And I don't understand it as I've never asked for a penny off him and never got anything.

Tamsin, who was pregnant with her second child and had a two-year-old daughter, said of her daughter's father: 'My [ex-]boyfriend has not helped at all, he's a waste of space… He hasn't been interested in his daughter unless it is to spite me.' Holly felt that her partner, the same age as her, was just not mature enough to deal with the responsibility of parenthood:

He [partner] didn't want to take responsibility and he wanted to choose whether he wanted to be here or not… He's not really matured yet and he was just thinking about education and didn't want to think about anything else.

Claire talked of how when her son was born (two years earlier) his father took an interest and saw him every weekend, until he was three or four months old. Then the contact started becoming less frequent and Claire believed he made contact only because his own mother encouraged him to do so. Claire said that she continued to try to involve the father of her son and called him up when she knew she was pregnant with her second child. She said:

He asked why I had bothered calling him and I said, 'Because your son is going to have a baby brother or sister'. He has told other people that I stop him from coming to see him [his son] when all I have tried to do is get him to have his son more often

Marie talked about how she wanted the father of her baby to have regular contact with their son:

My ex [baby's father] has just gone three months without seeing him [baby] and now he has decided he wants to see him again…but since he was born he has never been that interested. It's disruptive to have him [baby's father] popping in and out.

Although some young women felt that they and their child received little support from a partner and felt negative, or at least ambivalent, towards them, other young women talked more positively; when a relationship was working well, the support of a partner was seen as invaluable. Amanda felt that her partner help the mainstay of her support: 'The only person that was really there through the pregnancy and birth was my boyfriend – none of my family were there.'

Colleen commented:

> He [boyfriend] has always been there for me. He tries to help me sort out any problems I may have or he'll just sit and listen. He helps as much as he can but lives [outside of the area]. He comes over nearly every night, when he can afford petrol. He bathes the baby, puts him to bed, things like that. If the baby wakes up, he'll go to him.

Importantly, support could also be derived from a new partner. After the father of her child had left, Donna said of her partner: 'I met my current boyfriend. He treats the baby as if it is his own and the baby loves him.' Similarly, Claire, Katie and Marie, since having their children, all talked of meeting new partners who were supportive, took an active involvement in caring for the children and provided them with space and time for themselves to have a break, as well as supporting them emotionally.

Georgia also talked about the difference it made having a caring partner with her third child, compared with there being no one there for her other two children, who were now in foster care. She felt that her partner's presence at the birth is why she felt more of a bond with her third child.

RELATIONSHIPS WITH FAMILY

When talking about 'family', young people mentioned a wide range of people. These included, for example, their own mothers and fathers, wider family members such as aunts and grandmothers, their current or ex-partner's parents, as well as foster carers and residential social workers.

Leticia described how the birth of her baby daughter had changed the nature of the relationships in her partner's family and the implications it had for her and her baby. Her daughter was afforded high status within her partner's family. Her daughter, she said, was considered to be her partner's mother's first grandchild because she was born to her (partner's mother's) son, even though she (her partner's mother) already had a granddaughter born to her own daughter. Leticia explained:

OK, so in the African way, they believe that the boy has the child more than the woman has the child. He's the boy and because he's the baby's father, this is her first granddaughter. 'Cos his sister has got a baby. It's not really, really hers. Because the other granddaughter [partner's niece] is looked upon as a Sierra Leone 'cos her dad's a Sierra Leone. Do you get it? It's the African mentality. So she [our daughter] is more Ugandan. That's what African people think 'cos the dad's from Uganda. And my mum is Ghanaian and my dad is Nigerian but she wouldn't be looked on as that. She will be looked at as more Ugandan 'cos her dad's from Uganda.

Young people spoke about the relationships with family members sometimes ambivalently (family members were perceived, on the one hand, to be supportive, yet, on the other hand, their involvement was viewed with suspicion) and sometimes negatively (in that family members provided little or no assistance). Yet, family members had also provided different sorts of support – financial, emotional and practical (such as childcare) – and these sorts of help were spoken about positively by young people.

Young people's ambivalent feelings regarding family members were, on occasions, related to their family's greater interest in the baby rather than in them as a young mother or father. Siobhan said:

My stepmum and dad sort of disowned me…if I went down there they'd slam the door in my face and as soon as I had her I went down there and it was open arms, 'Come in'. It was awful, I preferred it when they used to slam the door in my face.

Mandy felt it was probably only the baby that kept her in contact with her own mother:

We were starting to build bridges; we forgot about the past, but when I fell pregnant, she [mum] was there all the time…I think this is the only thing that really is keeping us together, but I don't care.

Despite hopes that a baby might bring him closer to his family, Jack had come to the conclusion that his family wanted only to see their granddaughter and were not supportive of him at all.

Young people also had mixed feelings about family members who, while initially supportive, became less interested as a baby became a bit older and the 'novelty wore off'. Serena commented: 'It's fine when they are babies, everyone wants to help but as soon as they grow and up and start picking things up and that, no one wants to help.'

One housing support worker also noted that young people sometimes regain contact with families once they have babies, only to be rejected once again: 'It's just new blood in the family and everybody is interested for five minutes.'

On occasions, 'in laws' could be somewhat overbearing if they became too involved. Bridget, who was living with her partner's parents when at 15 years old she had a son, appreciated the help she received but wished for more independence. She commented:

> His mum was a real help but a bit too helpful... She would step in all the time and take him off me even when I didn't want her to. I appreciated the help but wanted to be left to my own devices more.

Some young people spoke rather more negatively about their family members. Phoebe, who was 20 and had a two-year-old son, commented: 'I need to have a break from him [son] to sort my head out...but that is not going to happen. I am desperate for someone to step in and help, my mum wouldn't do it.'

Brandon, however, felt unable to share the news of his baby son with most members of his family because he had felt rejected by them, especially his grandmother:

> None of the family, my nan and everyone, know about their grandson...only my brother. My brother was really happy for me but I have told him not to tell my nan because she couldn't be a part of my life so she obviously can't do it for my son.

Jeffrey, who was 20 and had a seven-month-old daughter, talked about how his partner's mother was keeping him from the child, and he had to go to court to gain access to see his daughter:

> It's very hard to put into words what is going on at the moment...it's just everything that's happening. If her mum let us make our own decisions then we would be able to put it right. At the moment the court is the only option.

Some professionals and young people expressed concerns about the variable outcome of efforts to build bridges with estranged family members. A number of young women described particularly stormy and complex relationships with their mothers prior to becoming a parent so were understandably cautious about different responses to them once they became or were about to become mothers.

Other professionals talked about young people being removed from negative family relationships only to gravitate back to them once they left care. Once they had children, this was sometimes a cause of concern. One social services manager commented: 'Many young people have destructive relationships with families but have chronic attachment disorders, they cannot walk away.'

Although family members were sometimes spoken about ambivalently and even negatively, there were also numerous accounts of family members providing assistance, help and support. Young people sometimes spoke of ongoing support and, on other occasions, of relationships changing for the better.

Colleen said that her father helped her out when she was 'stuck for money' or if the baby needed something. and her mother would assist with childcare and give her a break every couple of weeks. Fran, who had ended up living with her (parents') neighbours before she was pregnant, had experienced a 'relationship breakdown' with her own parents. The neighbours continued to be a source of support since having her son. In addition, although her grandmother had been upset and 'rejected her' when Fran told her she was pregnant, she later bought things for her son and supported her emotionally too.

David talked of the hopes and aspirations that his family had for him to have children and 'settle down'. As he explains, hearing that he was going to be a dad at such a young age did not come as a shock to his family:

> When I first told my mum [about the baby], she was mad at first and then OK. My mum was 16 when she had my brother, 19 when she had me. My brother was 14 when he had his kid, and my cousin was 15. My older sister got pregnant when she was young too. My mum wants me to settle down with my new girlfriend, get a nice flat, a nice cosy life with kids.

Katie said that, since having her baby, she was getting on much better with her mother who she described as her main source of support. Sonia also commented:

> Me and my Granny [main carer] get on better. We used to be at each
> other's throats all the time, but now she's my best mate because she wants
> to help the baby and she just loves him. I didn't think she thought I was
> responsible or anything before.

Partners' families variably provided financial support, equipment such as
a buggy or a cot for the baby, occasionally provided a chance of a holiday
or gave direct support and guidance to young parents about how to care
for the baby.

Where there was no direct contact with birth families, young people
talked about receiving ongoing support from foster parents and residential care homes with whom they continued to maintain contact. Mandy,
for example, said:

> I've always relied on the home [residential care home], the social worker
> and the leaving care worker are my family… I went to this one thing, but I
> couldn't sit there because I didn't feel comfortable talking to anyone… So, I
> just relied on the home and social services.

RELATIONSHIPS WITH FRIENDS

Although neither partners nor family, friends were almost always
spoken about positively. Most young women said they received most
support from friends who were also pregnant or parents themselves.
Amy felt that she had lost contact with most of her friends, leaving only
the ones that had children themselves. Amy and Serena, like a number
of other young women we spoke with, also described how they had
friends who had also been with them in care and had gone on to have
children of their own. Serena found she got a huge amount of support
from her friend from care and said: 'You can talk through your problems
with her and she understands.'

Colleen said of her friends:

> One has a baby the same age as [my baby], another is just about to drop;
> it's nice to have something in common. I don't see them that often but
> when I do they are very supportive. We have a laugh. The girl I live with,
> she's got a baby too, we get on really well, she's brilliant. We help each
> other out with our babies.

On the whole, friends featured as a central part of many young women's support networks. They would help with childcare, be supportive emotionally, and were people you could share experiences with and seek advice from. Interestingly, many young people described the new friendships that they had developed since becoming pregnant or having their baby. This was often as a result of the accommodation they were placed in. Friendships made in mother and baby units or other supported housing facilities, for example, were common.

BEING A PARENT: FEELING PROUD

We asked young people what they liked about being a mum or a dad. Bridget, aged 17 at the time of the research, and who had her son when 15 years old, stated, 'I like all of it' and, although it was 'hard at times', there was nothing that was a major problem. Bridget was living with her son's father and commented: 'things are going well, he [partner] has a job, we've just moved into this new flat which we are doing up [after living in temporary accommodation].' And Poppy's response was: 'It's very rewarding. The first smile, the first word, it's adorable, I love it. It's a lot of hard work but…'

For many, the sense of achievement they felt as their children grew and developed was evident. When we asked Claire what she enjoyed about bringing up her two-year-old daughter and three-month-old son, she said:

> The cuddles, and seeing the way my son is with his new baby sister. He helps with everything and when she's asleep it's our time… seeing him feed himself now and he loves drawing, he holds his own pen, he is a little boy now and not a baby any more…seeing him laughing.

Amy, who had a three-year-old son, having become a mother when she was just 15, said: 'I am really proud of my son and of myself and the way I've brought him up and the fact I've done it myself.'

Although more likely to depict less straightforward experiences of fatherhood, young men, like young women, frequently expressed their excitement at becoming fathers. Jack enjoyed watching his daughter, aged four at the time of the research, progress and seeing her attend nursery but described how he felt very protective towards her and was emotional whenever his daughter became upset or vulnerable. He commented: 'Some parents say go to school, no matter what. I will stay with my daughter and help her out.'

Danny, just 15, said: 'It's my baby isn't it…just looking at it and thinking it's mine and that.' James, who was aged 22 and had a four-year-old son, similarly commented: 'When I am with him, there is no other feeling, like it is great.'

Many young people suggested that they wanted to offer their own children a happier and better childhood than they themselves had. Brandon reflected on the type of relationship he wanted with his son, compared with the one he had with his own father:

> When I was little, I never had my dad about… I'm there a bit more, I am there for the little one and I will always be there until he is older… My dad only took up with me when I was 13, [now] I see my dad as a friend, but I don't want my son to see me as a friend – I want him to see me as a dad.

Brandon also went on to make an important point about how, if he had other children, having them within the same family unit was really important to him:

> I would like to have more kids…two or more. I want it to be with the same baby mother 'cos now I have had one of my kids with her, I want the other kids [with her]. Even if we didn't stay together I want to have all my kids with one mother. I want the brothers and sisters to group up in a family…not separated with different families. I want to make sure that my family is tighter than tight. I want them to look after each other.

CONCLUSIONS

Throughout this chapter we have described how young people viewed their lives as parents and the types and sources of support (or the lack of it) they received from partners, families and friends.

For most young people we spoke with, becoming a parent (in much the same way as becoming pregnant) was a time of change – an opportunity to reassess their lives and orient it towards caring for a child. They recognised and were generally able to respond to the responsibility of having a child. However, a number of them also faced new challenges too – coping with restricted time for leisure being one of them.

For some of the young men, being in trouble with the law and being in custody, difficulties in sustaining a relationship, and concerns about whether they were actually the father of the child were ongoing problems. Most, though, wished to be good fathers, and hoped they could support their partner and child emotionally and financially.

For some of the young women, post-natal depression and violence were particular problems. Although young women's current partners were sometimes violent towards them, a number of young women had been able to move away from violent relationships and some had found new boyfriends who were supportive of them.

Young women spoke about how some partners seemed unsuited as fathers – providing inconsistent care or none at all. Family members, too, could be less than helpful – some were uninterested, others interfered, yet others were uncooperative and unhelpful. That said, partners and family members could provide assistance that was reported to be of great help – emotionally, practically and financially. Especially for young women, friends, too, were reported to be people who could provide help and who 'understood'.

Overall, young people spoke positively about being parents – they were proud to be so and many felt a sense of achievement in their new role as a mum or a dad. They were determined, as far as circumstances would allow, to provide more for their children than they themselves had when growing up.

In the chapters which follow, we look at the support that was and was not available to young people from a range of social care, housing, education and health services. We report on the types of services and support that helped them and those that did not, and draw some conclusions about the implications that these findings have for policy and practice with respect to supporting young parents from care.

CHAPTER 8

FINDING A BALANCE: YOUNG PEOPLE'S EXPERIENCES OF CHILD PROTECTION PROCEEDINGS

I just needed someone to be on my side.

INTRODUCTION

When talking with young people and professionals, one area of practice was raised, time and time again, as a matter of particular concern – namely, child protection assessments. The aim of these assessments, which are normally carried out by social work professionals before and after the birth of the baby, is to establish whether there are any factors in the young person's life or circumstances which might present a risk to the safety and well-being of the child.

During interviews, however, we found that young people, as well as professionals, expressed concerns as to whether decisions regarding child protection assessments on children of young parents from care were conducted fairly, without prejudice and adequately resourced.

YOUNG PEOPLE'S PERSPECTIVES

Overall, young people indicated that child protection assessment processes were frequently confusing and at times frightening. Most young parents who spoke with us believed that, as young people who had been in care, they were more likely to undergo an assessment process than other young parents, and that this would be based on an assumption that they were unable to cope as parents. Pre- and post-birth assessments were, as a result, often perceived to be 'testing grounds', and a number of young people described situations where they felt confused and alienated by social workers or the social care system.

In general, young parents were hesitant in asking for support from social services. Some felt that the assessment process was weighted to 'set me up to fail'. Among other young people, Lucy commented that she felt watched 'all the time' and commented that assessments often took place in assessment centres away from any 'real' environment.

Mandy was 17 years old at the time of the study and her daughter was just 11 weeks old. She described how she was having an assessment by her social worker and resented the fact that she was treated differently from other young people:

> She [social worker] is doing an assessment but I find she asks us questions that she doesn't really need to know about. And she'll phone and say when is a good time to come round, and I say Friday or Tuesday afternoons is the best time to catch up with us and she'll come on Wednesday, and I had plans all day. So I had to cancel all me plans and I was really annoyed, and felt she was getting in the way. I think she [area team social worker] comes here because I have been in care. I've got a friend and she was my age when she had her baby, but she didn't have no social workers doing an assessment. Just because I have been in care doesn't mean I need to be assessed; because if I hadn't been in care there wouldn't have been no assessment. If we are getting them because we've been in care, if we've got to have them, then everyone should have one, we are just the same people.

When she spoke with us, Lucy was living with her partner, Chris, and they had a son who was eight months old. Lucy had undergone a pre-birth assessment which she felt was due mainly to social services knowing that Lucy's mother was a drug user. Lucy described how Chris had supported her throughout the pregnancy by working hard and providing everything that she and the baby needed. However, since he had used drugs in the past, he was assessed by social services throughout the pregnancy and after the birth of their son and had to go for routine drug tests. Lucy felt that Chris's willingness to agree to the drug tests was indicative of their commitment to ensure that their son was not brought up in an environment where there were drugs:

> he used to go for drug tests [urine tests done at the doctors] every two weeks as he had to prove to social services that he was not on drugs, and they all came back clear. He felt like me, that the baby was not going to be brought up in an atmosphere around drugs, like we'd been brought up in.

Chris also commented:

> I was taking drugs, smoking pot, until she was about three months pregnant. I got warned I might not be able to stay with the baby if I continued. I kept doing tests throughout the pregnancy but don't do drugs now. I am willing to do the test now if they want them.

After Lucy's son was born, and as a result of the pre-birth assessment, she was placed in an assessment centre, a placement she found particularly difficult:

> It was horrible, they just stuck me in there by myself and they [social services] never considered my feelings. I was there for 12 weeks but my boyfriend came in after 6 weeks. The woman I was living with at the supported housing had offered a placement as she had worked in residential care for nine years and the other [worker] was a qualified social worker and she said that she could have someone with me 24 hours a day to do the assessment. So I could have been in a place where I knew someone instead of a place where I didn't know anyone.

Other young people were also uncertain about who they could trust and confide in and felt let down by services that they thought they could rely on. Sian, whose son was taken temporarily into care, described how she felt let down by her family support worker:

> I saw her [family support worker] as a friend and told her everything... But I realised in the end that everything that I told her was brought up at the case conference and used against me... She stabbed me in the back really. I didn't have other people to talk to – I was on my own with [my son], I didn't see mum or dad ...so I saw her as a friend...that's why I can't trust them no more.

Phoebe, who was 20 years old when she spoke with us, had a two-year-old son. She raised concerns about her health visitor who, rather than supporting her, had, she felt, created further difficulties:

> I can't get on with my health visitor. She does my head in. I try telling her things and she just twists everything around. She's constantly in my life at the moment – ringing up every day and I don't like it. ...she got social services involved.

For a number of young people, the fact that they had heard about the likelihood of assessments and the fact that social services were associated with having the power to remove their children generated fear and mistrust, and served to further alienate them from the services available. Siobhan, who was 18 years old when she had her daughter, described the anxiety she felt soon after her birth:

> After she was born, they said she had to go into an incubator. I was petrified, I thought they were just trying to take her off me. I waited for two hours and then ran around the whole hospital looking for her... I was just paranoid, I know how my social worker works. She is a nasty person.

Sally, who was 17 years old when she spoke with us, had a 16-month-old son. She described how she had found the relationship with social services very difficult: 'They [social worker] were really horrible to me after he was born. They threatened to take him off me when I hadn't done anything. They was really getting on to me instead of helping me.'

When asked why she thought the social worker had responded in this way, Sally explained that she had been through what she described as 'a violent relationship' with her boyfriend. As a result she had left the relationship and had gone back to live with her foster parents. However, the relationship with her foster carers subsequently broke down because 'they were really digging into me all the time'. It was only at the point when Sally left her foster family and was effectively homeless that the social services department became aware of the violent relationship with her ex-partner. She explained: 'I had actually moved out of that violent relationship, they would never had known it had happened.'

Having deliberately removed herself from a relationship which constituted a threat to her and her son – and so having eliminated the risk to her son's well-being – Sally felt that she was being punished by the social worker for acting appropriately. As a result, her son was placed on the child protection register and assessed as being at risk of physical abuse. When we spoke with her, Sally's son no longer had an allocated social worker and had been removed from the child protection register. But, in order to achieve this, Sally had had to attend several review meetings. Sally spoke of her general feelings about the child protection assessment process she had been through:

> I hated it. They were making me feel depressed because they was always saying how unimportant I was. I mean I know he [the baby] is more important but they always made me feel so unimportant that it got me down.

Some young people stated that they would rather cope 'on my own' than involve a worker from social services. Phoebe commented:

> Social services have been on my case in the past but they were pleased with me when I was pregnant. If I needed support, they would open up my case again but I just tend not to involve them. I am just scared to go up to them – I don't like asking for help as I would rather sort it out myself rather than getting anyone else involved – I think it is my mess – I've got to deal with it.

Yet, as Phoebe spoke with us, she indicated that she was not coping as she had no support from her family, her partner or from any services. She was also very anxious about the behaviour of her two-year-old son and wondered whether he might have ADHD. Despite her anxieties about involving the social services department, she went on to say that she had in fact asked them if she could have a support worker, 'someone to take me out and talk to me...because I really need it'. This had been two weeks earlier and Phoebe had heard nothing since. In her desperation she had made an appointment with her GP the day after she took part in the study. Asked how she thought the GP could help, she commented: 'Just someone to talk to really...I don't really want to go on antidepressants because they just muck up my mind and I don't want to be relying on them the whole time.'

Young men who spoke with us also expressed reservations about involving workers from social services – although perhaps less often than the young women. James, for example, was no longer with his partner and, if he wanted to see his son, he had to go to where she lived. He was concerned about the well-being of his son because his ex-partner's new boyfriend was 'a drug user and is always pissed'. Yet, largely due to his own past experiences, he was reluctant to alert the social services department about his concerns. He explained: 'I can't tell social services anything as they will do nothing or just cause more problems. I do not want him [baby son] taken away from his mum as I know how it feels.'

Four of the young people who spoke with us described themselves as having some form of learning disability, including two with ADHD, one with combined dyslexia and behavioural problems, and another with general learning problems. Two of these young people's children had been taken into local authority care.

Theresa, who was 19 years old when she spoke with us, stated that she was coping with the aftermath of having her two-year-old daughter taken away and placed for adoption. Theresa told us that she had been diagnosed with having ADHD. She described how the decision had been made to take her daughter away from her after several court cases and attempts at foster placements, a time that had been very traumatic for her. She felt that she had neither been given a chance (she said that her last foster placement had been 'working very well'), nor provided with support once her baby had been taken away.

Taken together, young people's views of child protection assessment procedures were almost wholly negative. Yet, as Sally noted, what she had felt to be of greatest help was when her capabilities as a mother were recognised. Although she had found the assessment meetings intimidating at first, she spoke of the latest meetings as being more positive and even affirming. As Sally commented: 'They said I am a good mum.'

PROFESSIONALS' PERSPECTIVES

Several professionals we spoke with were aware of the challenges that young people faced when confronted with child protection assessment procedures. They noted that young parents from local authority care were often placed under greater scrutiny than other young parents. In turn, this could affect the extent to which they were willing to access local support services.

As one social worker put it: 'Young people with experience of being in care are under the microscope more so than any other teenage parents, which is not necessarily fair.'

A project development worker for a national charity providing support to young people leaving care described what he had observed in the assessment of one young woman: 'From the moment the baby was born, they started to collect evidence…she was under scrutiny right from the beginning.'

A teenage pregnancy coordinator observed:

> Being able to maintain control is more of an issue for young people in the care system. Having to jump through hoops has a knock-on effect when making decisions about their own pregnancy. Being judged about their parenting ability and being watched more carefully are factors in how young people view support as conditional and therefore it influences their attitudes towards getting support for their pregnancy and accessing services.

A senior social worker confirmed that young people's anxieties had a negative impact on their engagement with support services: 'A lot of young mothers are not very keen on social workers giving them support. Their view is that they will interfere and take their child into care.'

Professionals were aware, too, that young people may not fully understand either the processes associated with child protection proceedings, or their consequences. An educational support worker for looked after children talked about the impact of a child protection assessment for one young woman:

> My view would have been more to try and support her in looking after the baby even though there were other issues. She [young mother] thought the issue was that she slept a lot and because she had the baby in bed with her and she might roll over and kill it. If there were other reasons, she did not understand them. The thing that hurt the most was that the baby was going to be put up for adoption, and she never understood the implications of that, that she would never see the baby again.

Professionals also spoke of their concerns about what they saw as an unreasonable basis on which child protection decisions were made. One leaving care personal adviser, for example, talked about how she had challenged a request for a referral to the child protection assessment team for a young woman she hardly knew. She had refused the request on the grounds that she had not worked with the young woman for long enough in order to make a fair assessment and asked for more time. This extra time had enabled the young woman to 'turn things around' and change how she was perceived as a parent.

> I told her [young mother], 'I'll give you three months to show me that you are stable, and show them [senior managers] that you are stable'. And she came through well, she was able to show that she can do stuff, she got the support of other staff as well, their views were changed about her.

Another leaving care social worker highlighted how hard some decisions can be when it comes to trying to keep young mothers with their children. She described a not uncommon situation in which domestic violence and the risk to the well-being of the mother and the child were primary concerns:

> One young mother who is pregnant and her partner is being really violent, I know she will be a good mother and am being told that she needs to be child protected. The problem is the baby would then go on a register even before it is born...then she will lose the baby. I know that when she is not pregnant she will slap him back.

Professionals were generally aware that poorly made decisions could have a major impact on the lives of young people. Across all study sites, they described a relatively common scenario whereby some young parents failed to demonstrate that they could competently care for a child, had their baby taken into care and then subsequently became pregnant again soon after the removal of the child. This cyclical pattern of assessment and care posed a major challenge for their professional practice. This sequence of events was most commonly observed where young people had some form of learning disability. One social worker talked of how one young woman had given birth five times. With each child a care order had been placed on the baby before it was born, with the baby being subsequently removed immediately after the birth and placed for adoption. Each time the young woman soon became pregnant again, concealing her pregnancy as long as possible in an effort to be able to keep the baby. One leaving care manager noted:

> One 16-year-old mother became pregnant, [the] baby went into care and 12 months on she is about to give birth again. But she was so worried about losing it that she concealed and denied the pregnancy, which was

discovered when she was 37 weeks pregnant, just as she had the last contact with her first child.

Another consequence for parents who had their children removed from them related to drug use. A leaving care social worker described a situation in which two different young parents, both drug users, were clearly not going to cope. Going through repeated assessment processes had, she felt, merely 'prolonged the agony' for them:

> Two different social workers went in and said you have to jump through all these hurdles, and they were not able to do it and it prolonged the inevitable agony, and picking up the pieces after they had wheeled their babies away – they hit drugs big time then.

Notwithstanding this awareness of potential adverse outcomes, professionals commented on the challenges they themselves faced in finding an appropriate balance between the provision of support that would enable young families to stay together and the initiation of child protection procedures.

One factor influencing professional practice related to what some described as the 'drawback' of the government agenda to speed up the adoption process for young children. The result here, some commented, was that options for the interim care of a baby taken into care were reduced, as were the longer-term options for young parents who might require more time and preparation before being reunited with their children. Those most critical of this policy described it as a government 'band wagon' that had created conflict in local practice. One social worker said: 'There is [currently] a very strong drive towards immediate adoption but this limits the options.'

Another social worker commented:

> The Children Act says that it is paramount that we keep families together. The government says we have to adopt children as soon as possible. They are in direct conflict...but we do it, and because they [authorities] feel it is target led to get money – we don't have a choice, we need to adopt children much earlier...we put them through the system earlier. I have seen it where adoption goes horribly, horribly wrong.

A project development worker raised another important issue that emerged repeatedly as a theme – striking an appropriate balance between allocating adequate resources to enable professionals to assist young parents and the instigation of child protection proceedings. He reflected on the impact of this decision for one particular young woman:

> They [social services] have taken her child away into care. She loved the baby but there were not the resources there for her and it was not the fact that she was unable to cope. They offered her to live in a family assessment centre but it was a resource that was shutting down, so they then talked about moving her to another city. They were creating a situation that was going to fail.

Another factor that hampered professionals' practice was that – due to a lack of resources – they were not always in a position to provide the type of intensive support packages that some young people required. There was a general understanding among professionals that this could be a 'false economy', given the significant resources required in the medium to longer term to support a child through the care system. One social worker expressed her frustration in not being able to afford appropriate types of support for some of the young people she worked with:

> I have been in situations where I have tried to put an appropriate care package together, but it's impossible because there just isn't the money... Therefore, it's like a vicious circle... It's like you're in care, so your child will probably come into care.

Discrepancies between the support needs that are identified and the support actually provided were particularly apparent for young parents who had learning disabilities. One specialist leaving care personal adviser for people with a learning disability commented that young people with mild learning difficulties, having been through mainstream education and other services, often missed out on any specialist support as they left care, despite their heightened vulnerability.

One social worker talked about the potential of better outcomes for young parents with learning difficulties if they had more support:

> It's a bit ideal-worldish, but sometimes I think there needs to be more of a group situation where people with learning difficulties are almost in a situation with an adult carer, maybe to get through all the difficulties of the early years. Usually their heart is in the right place but they haven't got the necessary initiative to cope. I know people with visual and hearing impairments

do get by with support, so why can't that be the same for someone with learning disabilities?

A third factor, said to influence professionals' decisions, related to the assumptions that social workers might hold of young parents in or from care. While acknowledging that his views might not be shared by other professionals, one social services team manager believed that that there was a need to move from the 'knee jerk' reactions to intensive work with individuals: 'We are not going to stop young people being parents. We need to put young people into a non-threatening environment and look at the responsibility of having children on an equal footing.'

A number of professionals described the negative assumptions made about whether or not a looked after young person would cope as a parent, and how this could at times affect the course of action taken. A foster care manager stated:

> Maybe it's also a bit to do with the district social worker having a lot more faith in the young people or believing it can work. If the social worker thinks that the young person is never going to manage that baby and is going through the motions, when they make a mistake then the child is removed. They're almost waiting for it to happen... I mean maybe it wouldn't have worked anyway, but they need a bit of a life as well – being a young mum isn't just about having total responsibility for your baby.

However, holding more positive assumptions about young parents in and from care could, some professionals noted, be rather too close to operating with the so-called 'rule of optimism'. Aware of findings such as those contained in the Laming Report, there were said to be particular risks in being over-optimistic about the capacities of young people.[1]

Rather than holding positive assumptions or working under a 'rule of optimism', one professional stated that much could be achieved by creating transparency – and so trust – in the child protection assessment process. She provided an account of this:

> A young mum who was in care, and the child was in care because she hurt him, was then moved into foster care with the child. Then from there she

---

1   The Laming Report was a result of the independent statutory inquiry set up to investigate the circumstances leading to the death of Victoria Climbié in 2000 and to recommend action to prevent a similar tragedy happening again

went to a family centre. And part of the programme was that she had to attend here [the teenage parenting programme]. She has now attended for 18 months, her child is off the child protection register and she has her own accommodation. She now enjoys being a parent. [Before] she was in a family centre, but here she felt there was trust. We didn't do anything without talking to her first. We supported her and attended all her case conferences. She saw all the reports before we read them at the case conference. She actually said that she didn't feel 'false' here, whereas she had to continually put on a front when she was at the family centre because she felt she was being watched. They see it [the programme] as very different from social services, we don't make any decisions for them...they have to make decisions for themselves. If there is a child protection issue then we would encourage a young person to phone social services themselves, and if they don't then we would invite social services in.

CONCLUSIONS

In this chapter, we have outlined young people's and professionals' views of the child protection assessment process. On the whole, young people held negative views about child protection proceedings. They felt they were subjected to too much scrutiny and, having been in care, they felt that professionals judged them – and their ability to parent – unfairly. Instead of helping, professionals were seen to hinder some young people from 'getting on' with learning to be a parent.

Many professionals, too, indicated that young parents in or from care were placed under greater scrutiny than other young people. This was not necessarily unhelpful in itself. But taken together with other factors – such as operating with less than constructive assumptions of young people, restrictive national guidelines on adoption, as well as a lack of resources – could result in young parents feeling disadvantaged through child protection procedures rather than helped.

There was little evidence of professionals consistently building on the strengths of young parents – although one example of making the child protection assessment more transparent appeared to help one young person build trust in the process. In the next chapter, we report on young people's experiences of a range of other services once they became parents, other than those related to child protection. These seem to suggest that some professionals, at least, may be developing a mode of working with, and engaging, young parents from care which is more likely to enhance their capabilities and their sense of well-being than the approaches described in this chapter.

CHAPTER 9

GETTING HELP FROM SERVICES

I am just left on my own now to deal with it – and it's quite hard.

INTRODUCTION

From the time when they became parents, many of the young people we spoke with came into contact with a range of formal statutory and voluntary services. These included housing, social services, leaving care services, foster care, primary care services, childcare support, education and advice about employment, grants and benefits. Young people said that they wanted services that helped them practically – such as providing them with a safe place to live – as well as emotionally – such as having someone to talk to and share their experiences with. In this chapter, we describe young people's experiences of a range of social care (including leaving care), health, housing and related services once they were parents. Drawing on what young people told us, we conclude by outlining some of the qualities of the sorts of services that are most likely to be of use and relevance to young parents who are, or have been, in care.

HOUSING

Young people stated that living in secure, stable and safe accommodation was fundamental to their ability to cope, manage and do well as parents.

Many young people talked about their increased vulnerability and insecurity as a result of not having permanent and adequate housing for themselves and their children. Several young women had been sexually assaulted in temporary accommodation placements – in one case this assault was witnessed by a young child. Others described accommodation that was dirty, in locations where they felt vulnerable and unsafe and where there was widespread drug use – environments unsuitable for raising children. Marie described how she lived with her five-month-old son in bed and breakfast accommodation:

> I was in a B&B for three months. It was horrible, it wasn't really a B&B it was a room in a shared house – shared kitchen and bathroom. My son was five months old. It was awful, there was no room.

When we talked with Phoebe, she had lost the tenancy on her flat and was living with her two-year-old son at a friend's house. Sarah spoke about a time when she was in bed and breakfast accommodation and not being able to have her children with her; she had to leave them with friends.

Poppy commented on how the type of accommodation that she was forced to accept affected her chances of providing a safe place for her child:

> You have this responsibility to make sure that your child comes into a safe home. I was in a hostel and then I moved to this mother and baby hostel, it was like a drug house…it was disgusting…rats and mice and ants…I begged everyone to move me on. In the end I was lucky enough to have a decent social worker and a decent council worker.

Uncertainties about the permanency of accommodation were raised as a problem by some young people. Fran commented on the fact that she was completely unsure about how long she would stay in temporary accommodation with her one-year-old son. In the mean time it was not possible to make it her own or decorate it as she wished; she commented 'for all I know I could get a letter [from the local authority housing department] in the next three or four weeks or I could hear in three or four years' time'.

Jack, who was no longer living with the mother of his four-year-old daughter, talked about his frustrations with a bureaucratic and complex housing allocation system. At the point at which he took part in the research, he had had his application for accommodation turned down again. He commented: 'There is a maze of doors to go through to try and get accommodation and yet there are hundreds of houses around that are all boarded up.'

Young people who had access to good quality supported accommodation tended to view this positively. Hostel staff were described as being supportive in housing tribunals and helped with practical skills, such as helping them to learn how to cook. Some young people also described occasions when hostel workers accompanied them to look at more permanent accommodation and acted as advocates if they felt they were being 'pressurised' to accept inappropriate housing. Having experienced this type of support from workers in the hostel where she stayed with her young baby when she was 16 years old, Ese made the following recommendation:

> If they've got a baby I think they should wait like everyone else in temporary accommodation. Just as long as it is good temporary accommodation. I don't think that the government should be allowed to put these young teenage mothers into flats, in the middle of a bad estate where it's damp and there are broken windows. I think there should be someone there, to go with them to see the property. And if it's not right, [then] someone should fight the case with them. Because that's why they accept it because there's no one there to fight the case with them and that's where they start having a bad life.

Some supported mother and baby units were viewed particularly positively by young people. Colleen was in a housing association mother and baby unit and said:

> Since I've been here I've felt more confident with doing things. They do help. No matter what they are doing, unless they are already helping someone else they will just drop it. Even if it is really important paper work, they will just drop it and help you. I think it's brilliant. They really make you feel at home.

Rosie, looking back on her experiences of a unit run by another housing association, said:

> The unit I used to be in was great. It was safe and they showed you how to do things. Like I didn't know how to manage my money properly [before],

but within a month of being there I could do it. I was there less than a year and moved out a month before her first birthday.

One specialist teenage midwife echoed the views held by some young people:

> I think a good thing for young parents leaving care are the mother and baby units. They seem to be a positive thing. They need a balance in between, rather than stepping out on their own. They need someone who is there but not standing over you. Most of them seem to welcome that.

However, other professionals felt that while they suited some young parents others were less likely to want to stay in mother and baby units. In some units, for example, staff refused to allow partners to stay over or be involved with the children. For some young people, 'floating support' was thought to be a suitable option.[1] This had the benefits of enabling assistance to be provided according to need, and through housing associations which were not, as one worker put it, 'tagged to social services and all the baggage that entails'.

The location of housing was very important and, where there was a shortage within an authority, this meant that some young people were placed in districts away from family and friends. Sally explained that, although she had been moved for the 'safety' of herself and her young son, she felt that the change had in fact heightened her vulnerability:

> They sent me to a place away from where I lived with my foster parents. I was on my own, I didn't know anyone, I didn't have a television, I didn't have a cooker. It was the weekend my ex-boyfriend came out of prison, so I was very scared…but they wouldn't let me transfer back to where I had lived before, where all my friends and family could support me.

One Sure Start Plus adviser talked about how social isolation was often caused through housing allocation. Even though the housing provided locally was of a high quality, it could often be on a geographically isolated estate with poor public transport, away from family and friends. Her experience was that unless young women were linked into appropriate services, they were likely to become isolated and have limited options:

---

1   'Floating support' is provided to young people wherever they are living, rather than being provided as part of an accommodation package.

> If the mothers are given support, brought into contact with other people and given the occasional night off with a babysitter, it can make a big differ-ence, they don't get depressed and they start to realise that there are a variety of choices that they can make, and they are more confident in deciding on different options for themselves.

While poor housing created particular problems for a young mother and her child, fathers, too, spoke about how inadequate accommodation made it difficult for them to bring up their children as they wished. Alex talked about how he could not have his children to stay if he was living in a hostel or on the streets and he felt strongly that services were generally designed to support mothers and not fathers:

> I was on the streets at a time when me and my ex were talking and getting on OK, and she was going to offer me to have the kids every couple of weeks... But I only had the hostel or night shelter. They won't give me a council property so that I can have my kids. It's a catch-22 situation with the government... If you are young, single and a father you don't get anything... If you are young, single and a mother you get everything... There's nothing on offer for the father.

SOCIAL SERVICES

Young parents had contact with social services and social workers for many reasons – not only for child protection assessments. Most young people we spoke with had been in contact with social services depart-ments for many years, this beginning when they were young children. Many young people had been in contact with a series of different social workers and/or had been in a number of care placements. For some, these earlier experiences influenced how they felt about engaging with social services and social workers as parents. Mary, who was 20 years old when she spoke with us, and who had the first of her two children when she was 16 years old, stated: 'I never liked social workers and never got anything off them and just wanted to be treated like a normal parent who hadn't been in care.'

Some young people felt that social services staff engaged differently with them once they had a child. Before having children, a number of young people, particularly young women, talked about asking for, but not receiving, support from social services. After having a child, the attention of social services was described as almost predatory. Siobhan expressed this particularly vividly:

> Social services were no help. They didn't lend me any money, they didn't put me in contact with anybody I could talk to…they just sat back and waited until I had had her…and then they all came swarming in and took over sort of thing… At the time, she didn't feel like she was my baby, it just felt like she was everyone else's baby…all the social workers were butting in and my family was telling me what to do… I just didn't think she was mine.

Some young people were troubled by the lack of concern that social services staff appeared to have for their own needs as young parents and they saw social services staff as being concerned only for the welfare of the child rather than for the child and her or his mother. Sally felt that once social services had been satisfied that her son was safe in her care, they no longer seemed to be bothered about what happened to her. She commented:

> Since social services have stopped nagging me [monitoring the baby], I am getting no support now, no advice on things I want to talk about. I am just left on my own now to deal with it and it's quite hard.

Yet, despite the frustrations that many young people described with 'regular' social workers or social services departments, they had a very different perception of a new type of professional who was gaining credibility among young people at the time of our study – the leaving care worker.

LEAVING CARE SERVICES

Unlike social services, very few young people commented negatively on leaving care services.[2] For one young person, Simone, who did criticise the service, this was because the visits from her leaving care worker

---

2   In two of the areas where we conducted the study, some leaving care services had been set up prior to the Children (Leaving Care) Act 2000. In these and other study sites, new or extended services were under development. This meant that not all young people had access to leaving care workers, or were in the process of being allocated a leaving care worker.

ceased just two months after she moved to her flat. At this point, she felt very much on her own.

> Once I was in, it was 'there you go', no one was coming round or phoning or writing letters…'there you go, get on with it'. You've got to work out your bills, things you've never done before, managing to budget money. It was a very hard time.

Far more common, however, were positive reports of leaving care services – with the work of staff being compared favourably to those in social services. Katie felt that, while 'social services haven't really done nothing', the after care team had 'helped a lot. We have talks, [he] helps us with debt and stuff, anything I need help with'.

Where the leaving care service was well established and well known, young people frequently described the holistic nature of the support they derived from their leaving care worker, the fact that they were accessible, and that they were 'there for them' on many different levels. Jane said: 'They [leaving care service] are really helpful. I can talk to my worker about frustrations with the child and about positive discipline as I don't believe in smacking a child, and he gave me good suggestions for managing him.'

For Georgia, it was more than anything the attitude of her leaving care worker that she appreciated. Comparing her with earlier social workers, Georgia said: 'She didn't come across all hoity-toity like most of them are, they think they are above you, look down on you, think you are a piece of crap'.

For Serena, it was a combination of the practical support that was provided along with an empathetic and understanding approach that she felt able to relate to: 'She [leaving care worker] takes me shopping every week and helps with the decorating and with the child. A good worker is someone you can relate to and talk to, and they don't act like they know better.'

When it was required, the practical and tailored (sometimes intensive) support was invaluable for some young people such as Mandy:

> My leaving care worker came every morning for a few hours during the first few months after the baby was born, she would do the bottles, watch the baby while I was in the bath, do the shopping. Now they is going to help us

with a nanny during the day, just so I can have some time with me friends as well, because I am really lonely, 'cos I never see my friends.

Where services were provided through the voluntary sector, it was the neutrality of the service that some young people valued most. Siobhan, who was 18 when we spoke with her and had a ten-month-old daughter, said of her leaving care worker:

He came with me to all my antenatal classes... He used to stay with me for 2–4 hours at the hospital while they were doing my scans or whatever... They [voluntary organisation] gave the most support. If it weren't for them, I wouldn't have been able to keep [my baby]. Social services would have come and taken her off me.

Jasmine, aged 19 who had a two-year-old daughter who had been taken into care, talked of the support she had throughout the childcare proceedings from the same service:

I really liked [voluntary organisation leaving care service]. They help you...they are all there for you. You can go up there for a chit-chat...can go for my coffee... I can talk to them because I know them. I knew he [worker] would be there for me – he came to every [child protection] court case.

Professionals also commented on what they thought made leaving care services more responsive to what young people wanted and needed. As one leaving care manager put it: 'The really positive thing about leaving care is that the kids don't see it as part of social services, which they view negatively, and they see themselves at the steering wheel, planning their own futures.'

Another leaving care services manager described how additional resources (particularly in some authorities) enabled the provision of a much more intensive level of support:

The structure of the service is such that it allows more support to young people, particularly where there are complex issues. Here, we can jointly allocate a case between a social worker and a personal adviser [PA]. So the PA is able to do a lot more support work with the young person. I have great hopes and expectations of the role of the PA.

A manager of a relatively new leaving care service talked about the importance of being able to offer young people leaving care concrete things in terms of housing and benefits which they have typically had difficulties accessing in the past. He said:

> I am already getting some good feedback from young people that the service is OK, it already has a recognition by young people of being a positive thing. I say to them, 'I don't know what you have experienced before, but here it is different…we can help you'.

FOSTER CARE

Mother and baby foster care placements were, on the whole, valued by those young people who had experience of them. Such placements could provide ongoing emotional and practical support for new mothers and gave a sense of security and reassurance to young women in the early stages of being a mother.

However, despite the perceived benefits of these placements, there were some issues that were particularly difficult for both foster carers and young people to comprehend. These related to the role that the foster carer was expected to assume once the baby was born. While carers were expected to parent both the young mother and the baby, this sometimes put them in a difficult position and raised questions of how to provide adequate support to *both* the mother and the child.

For example, despite being very happy in her foster care placement and her foster carer providing what she saw as really good support, Michelle, who was 16 years old and had an eight-month-old son, felt that social services were not happy about this:

> She [social worker] says I should not let him [baby] go to the foster carer so much…but he hasn't got nobody else…so she says to her [foster carer] try not to help her so much…try not to be around [baby] so much…that is so annoying. She [social worker] claims she [foster carer] helps me so much they want to move me to a mother and baby unit to monitor me. I say if I'm there who's going to help me? When she had her children she had her family around helping… I haven't got the family so my foster carer is helping me…they are annoying…there won't be no one there [mother and baby unit] to help…then if I crack they are going to take him.

A major dilemma for foster carers was whether or not they were expected to adopt a supervisory role in relation to the young mothers who lived with them. As one foster care manager explained:

> Is the foster carer there to assess the parenting skills of the young person? Is she there to look after the baby or not? How do you define roles? It's very hard being a foster carer because you want to give young people a normal experience, and yet there are lots of rules and boundaries. Some carers don't want to 'grass them up' to the social workers because they know that they will see it as a significant thing that they didn't come home last night, and it will affect this young person's chance of keeping the baby…and that it can be as whimsical as the allocated social worker. If it was a different team and a different social worker then you might have a different response, the foster carer knows that.

In addition, there was some confusion expressed by foster carers as to whether a baby born to a young woman in foster care was in fact 'looked after', and what eligibility there was to receive support for the baby, the mother and foster carers. One foster carer described how this lack of clarity had been upsetting to both the young mother in her care, and their relationship. She felt that the local social services department had offered no additional financial support for the major changes to the house required to accommodate the young woman and her child, but instead placed extra demands on both the young mother and foster carers. She described the assistance provided by the social services department as 'intrusive' and 'heavy handed' rather than 'supportive' and, as a result, felt that the relationship between herself and the young mother had been damaged.

Foster carers also talked of the importance of giving more intensive and ongoing support to young mothers who were finding it difficult to cope as new parents. One foster carer reported still caring for the baby from a mother and baby placement, after the mother had just disappeared:

> The last girl [to have a baby] was the mother of the baby I have now – she came as a mother and baby placement – had possibly had a miscarriage or abortion prior to having baby and, whilst coming into foster care, she miscarried in the house. She still lives locally but never comes to see him. She

wasn't ever very responsive to the child, not at all affectionate. She went out for coffee one day and never came back.

However, this foster carer, at the same time as working with this young woman, had also been caring for a number of children on short-term placements, all of differing ages and all with highly complex needs – a situation which undoubtedly prevented her offering the type of intensive support that the young mother needed.

Sally also talked of how it would have been so much more helpful for her to have stayed with her foster carers for longer after having her son. However, after three months there was no more funding available to finance the placement. Although she could have left her child with the foster carers, she herself would have been unable to stay with him. Sally commented: 'It's hard looking after a newborn baby when you don't know anything about them.'

Several professionals highlighted the importance of striking a balance between allowing young parents to continue to enjoy their youth and promoting responsibility. The role of the 'corporate parent', for instance, was sometimes felt to be somewhat strict and inflexible in an effort to 'speed up' the transition to independence. As one foster care manager commented, it was always good to think about how you would resolve issues if the young people concerned were your own:

> If my daughter got pregnant, I would support her and let her go out – that's what normal families would do. Whereas, I think we're a bit prescribed about what we see as OK and if it was our own we would probably give them a lot more leeway and let them fail a bit more. They've got less time to succeed you see. They've got to go out at 18 years and be completely self-sufficient, I mean that's not normal any more – that's an artificial kind of cut-off point.

Those young people who were in foster placements at the time of the study derived much support from them. Jenny, who was 15 years old and had a 10-week-old son, talked about how happy she was that, at a permanency planning meeting, it was agreed that her and the baby could stay with the foster carer. 'Hopefully', she commented, 'We can stay until I go on to university'.

PRIMARY CARE SERVICES

As outlined in Chapter 6, the mixed experiences that young people had of primary care services throughout their pregnancies held true once they were parents, too. While some young people described having very positive relationships with GPs, health visitors and other primary care workers, many others expressed concerns about the stigma or lack of support or empathy they received. Serena commented:

> They think you are a paranoid mother because you are young. I don't like going to GPs myself. They don't treat young mums the same. They think you don't know much. I felt like he didn't listen to me properly and this needs to change.

For young people who experienced varying degrees of post-natal depression and/or anxieties, having access to sympathetic health services was particularly crucial. Some professionals felt that these feelings of depression were exacerbated by some of the specific pressures on young people from care. One teenage pregnancy coordinator commented:

> Post-natal depression is more common among these young parents, as they may be prone to having more fear about their own capabilities of being a good parent. They also fear the involvement of social services if they admit to having emotional difficulties.

Yet, although young people might have gone to a GP with such feelings, hoping for a sympathetic response, they did not always find this. Descriptions of GPs being dismissive of their feelings and symptoms were not uncommon. More importantly, there was a lack of sensitivity about the type of factors that might make some young people from care more likely to experience symptoms of post-natal depression than other young parents such as a lack of family support or uncertainties about accommodation or the future with their children.

CHILDCARE SUPPORT

The lack of affordable and accessible childcare that might enable young parents to access education, training and employment, or just to have a break every now and then, was often a concern expressed by young parents. While this can be a problem for any young parents without family members to support them, the need for good quality childcare for young parents from care was evident. The young people we spoke with had strong concerns about the quality of childcare, and were acutely aware of the vulnerability of their young children. They often stated that childcare provided by a registered childminder would not be an adequate guarantee for their child's safety. While there were subsidised childminding places in some of the study sites, many young parents were reluctant to use them. Jane, who had two children, said: 'I got offered money to pay for a registered childminder, but I don't know them and you hear so many stories about them. I prefer to leave them with friends and certainly not in a crèche.'

These concerns appeared to relate to anxieties about their young children not being able to articulate any negative things that might happen to them. Jane went on to say: 'My oldest goes to nursery, but he's older and can tell me if anything goes on there, whereas young children can't.'

Among some young people interviewed, there was also some confusion over the childcare support young parents were entitled to, and how to access it. Tamsin commented: 'I asked for help with childcare, but was told by social services that I wouldn't get it unless [my baby] had a social worker. I would never put her under social services.'

Young people's housing situation also affected their access to childcare. For young parents in temporary accommodation, for example, there seemed little point in reserving a nursery place, only to be housed subsequently outside of the area.

It could take time for some young people to develop trust and confidence in childcare services, but, once this was established, young people could benefit from them in other ways, too. Serena commented on how she valued the support from the crèche at a specialist education service for mothers and babies, but that it had taken time for her to feel confident with this service. She said: 'I've been going there since the baby was four months. When I first went there, no-one could tell what to do but now I can't stay away from three. The baby is happy there.'

Where childcare worked well, it appeared to be valued by young people. And, where it worked well, a degree of trust had been built up between the young person and the childminder. A teenage pregnancy coordinator commented on this:

> Young mothers need to feel confident about the quality of childcare. They need to feel able to visit different types of childcare provision and to choose what they think is the best for their baby. They need to be helped and empowered to take the step of entrusting someone else to look after their child.

EDUCATION, EMPLOYMENT AND BENEFITS

Of the 47 young women who spoke with us, four were in part-time employment, seven were at college, and a further three reported they were about to re-enter education – all of these young women had received specialist assistance through a teenage parent programme focusing on education and employment. Somewhat fewer than three-quarters of the young women received income support – and all of these hoped to re-enter education and/or training or employment in the near future. Of the 16 young men who spoke with us, two were in full or part-time employment, three were on training programmes, one attended university and three were in custody.

Although there has been strong government support in recent years for the provision of flexible learning opportunities for all young people and to widen opportunities to vocational and higher education, a number of difficulties remain for young parents from local authority care.

Several professionals commented that many young parents from care require additional parenting support and guidance, yet are encouraged to return to education with young children at the earliest possible opportunity. For some young parents like Rebecca, this posed something of a dilemma, because having time to build a positive and nurturing relationship with her pre-school children took priority over returning to education or training.

A number of professionals stated that, for young people who had not experienced positive parenting themselves, a return to education or training as soon as possible after having their children may not always be the best option. A manager of a voluntary sector parenting support project commented:

> I find this really difficult because I feel the teenage pregnancy unit [TPU] are focusing on getting the young people back into education as soon as possible, and getting their children into nursery and [this organisation] doesn't work like that. It works with letting them gain their parenting skills with the child... Because if you separate the two, the cycle will repeat itself, but if you can focus on the parenting skills and for the child to grow up with self-esteem and confidence, and value themselves, the cycle won't repeat itself – so it's quite difficult... I feel that we're actually working against the TPU.

Some young people noted that returning to education could be somewhat daunting. For Brandon, who was excluded from school aged 13, his long-term disengagement from education meant that returning to learning or training was not straightforward. He had no qualifications and was unused to studying.

However, most of the young people we spoke with aspired to return to some form of education or training in the near future. This was helped when, as in one study site in particular, a priority was given to educational provision for young people and when, as in two other study sites, flexible learning opportunities were provided. Providing an on-site crèche, alongside educational provision, and establishing links with Sure Start Plus facilities enabled some young parents we spoke with to access an extensive range of services on one site. That said, personalised support was seen to be needed if parents were to engage with educational opportunities. As one professional commented:

> The reticence that some young mothers feel is also countered by someone who will hold their hand and come with them for the first few times they go to a project to help them get over their initial fears. And it usually works. Once they get a taster and start to feel more comfortable they start to get enthusiastic.

With regard to benefits and grants, young people described how they were often confused about their entitlements. In making the transition from care to more independent living, and from not having a child to being a parent, young people said that they needed an understanding of, for example, balancing employment with entitlements such as the working family tax credit.

Moreover, young people said that they were uncertain, for example, whether and when young women were entitled to maternity grants, whether they should have additional support from the local authority social services department (to buy equipment for the baby) and how they made the transition to the benefits system once they were 18. These, and others, were all sources of confusion for young people with which they required assistance and guidance.

CONCLUSIONS

In this chapter, we have focused on the types of service provision that have helped and hindered young people in their new role as young parents. Central to them, they said, was secure and clean accommodation with at least a degree of permanency. While social workers were often spoken of as less than helpful, leaving care workers provided many of the young people with a relevant and timely service that often supported them practically as well as emotionally. In fact, young people particularly appreciated services that assisted them in being a parent: that is, services which did not focus solely on their child, but on them as a young person learning how best to be, and become, a young mum or dad. In the final chapter of this book, we draw together some of the lessons that the combined experiences of young people can teach us and outline the implications these lessons have for the development and provision of services for young parents in and leaving care.

CHAPTER 10

MOVING FORWARD

I don't know what I'm entitled to and what I am
not entitled to. As a care leaver, I need
someone that knows the system

When asked what would have helped her through some of the difficulties she had faced throughout her pregnancy and being a parent, Sally replied: 'Support really, a lot of support all the way. Young people don't get support when they are pregnant or when they've got a new baby or anything like that.'

In response to the same question, Phoebe spoke about how she had not expected to be bringing up her son on her own. Feeling let down by her ex-partner and her family, she was very clear about the help she needed on so many levels. She said:

> Do you ever feel sorry for people like me? I need someone to actually get me out of bed, to motivate me, to meet me, get me to do things, help me see things through. I don't know what I am entitled to and what I am not entitled to. As a care leaver, I need someone that knows the system.

Of course, not all the young people who spoke with us required the same degree of help as Sally and Phoebe. Many needed far less and a few needed a great deal more. But, if we think back to the various chapters of this book, we can see a number of ways in which focused service provision could have better provided for the young people with whom we spoke; during their early childhoods and times in care, throughout their pregnancies and once they became parents.

In Chapter 1, we set the context for the book by outlining some key literature regarding young people, young people in care and young parents. We provided an overview of the current policies and legislation relevant to the prevention of early pregnancy and the provision of support to young parents likely to impact on the well-being of all children and young people, and of young people in and leaving care. We concluded by noting the objectives of the research on which this book is based, outlining how the study was conducted and providing details of the young people and professionals with whom we spoke.

In Chapter 2, we presented a series of case studies to illustrate how, for Rebecca, Amanda, Lisa, Dave and Naomi, becoming a parent was one, albeit important, event in their lives that occurred among many others. By providing these case studies, we sought to demonstrate how young people's reasons for becoming pregnant, or parents when they did so, were relatively complex. There was a range of emotional, social and environmental factors that influenced their decisions and had an impact on their ability to parent their children successfully.

In Chapter 3, we highlighted how young people viewed their early childhood experiences and their lives in care. They spoke frequently about feelings of insecurity, of rejection and of being unloved. Being in care, some reported, tended to limit their opportunities in life and increased their vulnerability to a range of adversities, including violence, sexual exploitation and drug and alcohol use. What some young people did report to be of help, however, were care professionals who valued them as a young person, took an active interest in their lives and with whom they could develop and sustain a warm and caring relationship.

In Chapter 4, we focused on young people's accounts of how they learned about sex and relationships – as well as their use of contraception. For many young people, learning about sex and relationships appeared an almost serendipitous experience, in which young people tried to work out for themselves what they could more easily have learned through well-thought-out sex and relationships education. Young people frequently said that they would have benefited from more guidance from adults and professionals about their own physical and emotional development in general and about relationships and sex in particular. Professionals, however, appeared to find it a challenge to prioritise the timely provision of sex and relationships education relevant to young people's needs and circumstances.

In Chapter 5, we outlined the factors that influenced young people's decisions about the pregnancy. We highlighted the fact that they often lacked independent advice and guidance when deciding whether to continue with their pregnancy. More often than not, they felt under pressure to terminate a pregnancy – on some occasions from professionals and on others from family members. Young people themselves stated that, on the whole, they wished to continue with their pregnancy and were pleased that they had done so.

In Chapter 6, we focused on the meanings that young men and women gave to being pregnant and the prospect of becoming a parent. We reported on young people's accounts of informal support from partners, friends and family. In addition, young people spoke about rather more formal services and structures – some of which helped, while others were more of a hindrance and tended, they felt, to complicate their transition into parenthood. Friendliness, helpfulness, not being judgemental and proving to be trustworthy were all qualities of professionals which young people valued. Specialist teenage pregnancy midwifery services were, on the whole, liked by young people. However, insecurities associated with housing and pre-birth child protection assessments created particular anxieties for young people throughout pregnancy.

In Chapter 7, we turned to young people's perspectives on being a mother or father. Becoming a mum or a dad was, for those young people who spoke with us, a time of change. It provided them with an opportunity to look at their lives and identify new priorities associated with caring for their new daughter or son. However, there were also circumstances and issues that negatively affected their roles as parents, including post-natal depression, experiencing various forms of violence and relationship break-ups. Although not always the case, the partner and family members – and friends too – could provide invaluable support to young mothers. On the whole, young people spoke positively – even proudly – of their new responsibilities as parents.

In Chapter 8, we illustrated a particularly important, yet perhaps under-researched feature of being a young parent from care – their experiences of being subjected to child protection proceedings. Although acknowledged by some young people as important and occasionally helpful processes, for most, child protection proceedings were viewed as frightening and lacking in fairness. They left many young people confused and anxious and, at worst, resulted in them being harmed rather than helped, making them less likely to access support from services when they most needed it. Ensuring that child protection processes are more transparent, and that adequate resources are provided to identify and build on young parents' strengths and capabilities, may lead to fewer young people from care viewing them with such alarm and concern.

Finally, in Chapter 9, we highlighted the ways in which different types of social care, health, housing and welfare services provided – or failed to provide – the support that young parents said they needed. We reported on the importance of safe and secure housing for all the young people who spoke with us. Inadequate, inappropriate and unsafe accommodation created major obstacles for young parents leaving care, particularly since many had no dependable help available from families. In this same chapter, we also reported on what young people described as a particularly valued source of support and guidance, provided through evolving leaving care services. These were said to be set up in ways that increased day-to-day and direct assistance to young people. Moreover, a new type of professional – the personal adviser – was perceived by young people in a rather different way to other social services staff. In a relatively short period of time, leaving care professionals had, in some areas at least, gained the respect and appreciation of young people. It was a service that young people said they could rely on and trust.

A DEVELOPING POLICY CONTEXT

Given what young people have said, it seems reasonable to question whether teenage pregnancy, in and of itself, is necessarily a 'bad thing'.

When we consider the lives that many young people described prior to having their children, it is questionable whether parenthood, alone, limited their opportunities. Indeed, there appeared to be evidence to suggest that, for some young people at least, parenthood widened the opportunities available, helped young people to 'settle down', or helped them take a different and more positive pathway to the one they might otherwise have taken. Ultimately, for many young people we talked to, having a child had afforded them a degree of stability and focus to lives hitherto described by themselves as rather 'chaotic'.

It might be important to keep this in mind when considering the relevance of, for example, England's national teenage pregnancy strategy to the young people we spoke with. Providing good quality sex and relationships education, accessible and friendly information about sex, advice on contraception and guidance on the benefits of delaying parenthood are central to one component of the strategy.

Yet, the strategy appears to engage less fully than it might with broader issues that make the prospect of being a young mother or father more inviting than waiting for parenthood some years later. Feeling unloved and rejected, for example, not having a sense of belonging to a family, constantly moving home, sporadic attendance at school, experiences of abuse and neglect – these were just some of the childhood experiences of the young people who spoke with us. And, on growing older, these experiences may be compounded by others such as homelessness, problems with alcohol and drugs, domestic abuse and violence. Against this backdrop, it is quite plausible, even reasonable, to understand why having a child would be an attractive prospect and viewed not as a setback but as way forward.

There are, however, a number of changes to policy and practice that have occurred since 2002 and 2003 when we conducted the study on which this book is based. With regard to housing, for example, at the time of the study, the *Supporting People Strategy* (Office of the Deputy Prime Minister 2003) was about to be launched with its primary aim of ensuring that safe, secure and affordable housing was accessible to those who were most in need. Importantly, both 'teenage parents' and 'young people at risk' are identified client groups within the strategy. However, our study took place at a time when this initiative was not yet embedded in local authority practice. This may, in part at least, account for some of the accounts that young people gave of the inadequacies and insecurities surrounding their accommodation.

With regard to education – and since we undertook the study – there has been a growing emphasis on the educational attainment of looked after children and young people. The White Paper, *Care Matters: Time for Change* (DCSF 2007c), for example, outlines a range of measures to support the continuity and inclusion of looked after young people in education including extended support through personal advisers for young people who wish to pursue any training or learning opportunity up until the age of 25 years. At the same time, initiatives such as Care2learn have addressed some of the important barriers to education through providing grants to pay for childcare to enable the reintegration of young parents into education or training opportunities – although it should be said that this provision is currently limited to young parents under the age of 20 years.

Still, designing legislation and policy to protect young people from the negative experiences of childhood described in our study is far from straightforward. There is, however, every reason to think that the abundance of national strategies (outlined in Chapter 1) that cumulatively make up the Change for Children agenda in England may mean that future looked after young people have a wider range of choices and options and enjoy better quality care and support. It may also mean that, in times to come, they make different choices about pregnancy and parenthood to those made by the young people in our study. What we can say, however, is that the young men and women who spoke with us made particular decisions under challenging circumstances.

Given that these young people, and others, may continue for some time to choose to become parents at a young age, then our emphasis must surely be on maximising their opportunities as young parents and enabling them to parent successfully – which is, of course, a central plank in current UK policy. However, it was evident from our findings that generic services for young people require further sensitisation and understanding of the specific needs of looked after young people and those leaving care if they are to maximise their potential as young parents.

INFORMING PROFESSIONAL PRACTICE: FIVE KEY THEMES

Given what we have learned from the study, there appear to be at least five key themes which are as pertinent now as they were when we first spoke with the young people from care. Each of these themes, and the broader issues to which it relates, is important to bear in mind as services continue to be developed, implemented and reviewed.

The first of these is *transparency* of service provision. A lack of transparency was apparent throughout various aspects of young people's lives into and through the public care system. Decisions about moving young people into care or transferring them from one care placement to another, with little or no preparation or consideration for the impact on them, were experiences frequently described by respondents. Later on, young people reported that child protection procedures stood out as examples of services that lacked fairness and accountability to their needs as parents.

There was often confusion, too, over the rules and regulations that applied to young people's entitlements to benefits and grants, particularly as they moved into semi-independent or independent accommodation. At this point, what young people appreciated, however, were professionals who took time to explain the rules, regulations, processes and procedures attached to the provision of one or another service – and who spent time, too, checking with the young person that the reasons for a particular course of action were understood.

The second theme is that of *continuity of care*. The lack of such continuity hampered the lives, over many years, of those young people we spoke with. Whether it was the numerous changes in social workers, the overly frequent moves in placement – normally accompanied by a move to a new school – or, later on, having to move from accommodation to accommodation (often with very young children), these changes deprived young people of a sense of security and stability. Changes in staffing often left young people unable to establish the sorts of trusting relationships with professionals that underpinned a useful service.

In recent years, there has been an increasing recognition of the inadequacies of systems and services designed to support children and young people no longer able to live with their birth families. *Every Child Matters* and *Care Matters*, among other developments in policy, at least strive to promote continuity of care. Designated workers or personal advisers, sustained access to education, fewer placement moves and a greater degree of security and stability for looked after children and young people are now recognised as being a central part of securing 'stable relationships'.

The third theme we highlight relates to *adequate resourcing*. There were many occasions when more comprehensive and needs-led packages of support could have been provided to young people and young parents, if the necessary resources had been available. At the time of the study, a degree of energy and exitement surrounded the new leaving care services and their potential to improve the lives of young people. However, this new-found enthusiasm was somewhat dampened by concerns among professionals that the financial and personnel resources required to develop and sustain these services would not be available in the longer term.

'Significant extra resources' (DCSF 2008, p.3), around £280 million, are said to have been provided to the existing £2 billion plus to support those in local authorities and their partners to implement *Care Matters*. The themes of the implementation plan which are expected to guide work with children and young people in care are similar to those we identified through our study – including the need for consistency of care and providing young people with a voice.

Our fourth theme relates to children's and young people's voices and is that of *listening to what young people say* – and of responding to young people's identified (rather than assumed) needs, concerns and interests. As the implementation plan for *Care Matters* notes:

> To really make the difference, we all have to work harder to listen and learn from each other, to transfer our good ideas, skills and knowledge and always to seek out and listen to the voices of children and young people in care... Listening to the unique voice of every child in care is the only way we will be able to keep their individual and distinct needs in mind at every point. (DCSF 2008, p.1)

Young people's accounts of their experiences of times in care, pregnancy and parenthood, reported throughout the chapters of this book, were all too often fraught with examples of young people not being listened to, or, rather more seriously, of being excluded from involvement in making decisions about their own lives. As *Aiming High for Young People: A Ten Year Strategy for Positive Activities* (HM Treasury and DCSF 2007) notes, giving young people genuine influence over local services is the most effective way of ensuring better access to such services. Moreover, successful services and programmes involve young people in them, and all services should make a genuine effort to be sensitive and responsive to their needs and views.

Our fifth theme is closely related to listening and responding to young people and is concerned with *promoting and building on young people's strengths* – an issue we touched on in Chapter 1 of the book.

Over the years, the concept of a strengths perspective has been increasingly incorporated into the theory of social work practice (Saleeby 1996; Weick and Saleeby 1995). This perspective encourages professionals not to think in terms of individual, family or community deficits and problems but, rather more, to focus on potential strengths and capacities of the individual and those around them (Saleeby 1996). Such a shift in perspective can help to identify young people's potential and 'point to the kinds of interventions which may strengthen ... [their] participation in a range of learning communities and contexts' (Bottrell 2007, p.612). Young people's resistance to professionals' demands on them may well be a sign of resilience rather than a problem (Bottrell 2007). Provided with the right conditions, and even in challenging circumstances, young people can consolidate relationships and build trust among those close to them as well as identify new opportunities to 'get ahead' (Holland, Reynolds and Weller 2007).

In a similar vein, Gilligan (2001) has introduced a method of 'resilience-led practice' in social work which urges professionals to look at the wider social context of young people's lives and at what this might give them in terms of support. This approach assumes that young people have self-healing and self-righting capacities which can have a positive impact on their lives as long as they are provided with the right environments in which these capacities can thrive (Gilligan 2004).

Rather than focusing on the risks that young people face as a result of their current and past personal circumstances, this approach would attempt to balance these with personal strengths and other protective factors. Such protective factors may be drawn from a wide range of sources such as friends, family, education, social and community networks and professional organisations. Essentially, Gilligan's approach places responsibility on social work practitioners to position themselves in such a way as to be able to identify and release the positive processes in the wider context of young parent's lives that can assist them.

Such positioning requires the belief that a young person has the ability and potential (given the right support) to provide an acceptable quality of care to their children – one which at the very least is akin to what those who have not experienced the care system can provide. Simple though this may sound, some professionals may be somewhat blinkered by the negative influences that have dogged young people's lives prior to them becoming parents – influences that may limit their perceptions of young people and their potential to parent successfully. This matter is further complicated by the less than straightforward notions and understandings of what constitutes 'good' (or at least adequate) and 'bad' (or inadequate) parenting. Some research, for example, has shown that, in relation to teenage parents from care, the values and norms governing what is perceived as 'satisfactory' or con-versely 'unsatisfactory' parenting may be dictated by middle class princi-ples held by social workers and a generalised belief that parenting during teenage years is a bad thing (Rutman *et al.* 2002).

There were, of course, examples in our study, illustrated in this book, where young people did feel listened to, where they had a say in deci-sions that affected them, and where there was a sense that professionals and carers recognised their strengths and how these could be maximised. In quite a number of instances, it is important to note that it was volun-tary services that were able to work from a more strengths-based perspec-tive. We provided some examples of how these services were sometimes better placed and more able to critique, counter or mediate between some of the more procedural approaches to working with young people adopted through statutory services.

Indeed, there were occasions within statutory services, too, where building on young people's strengths lay at the heart of professional practice. There were reported to be leaving care workers, for example, who provided daily and continual practical and emotional support to young people. Specialist midwifery services were said to work with young women in ways which built their confidence and competencies. Young people also told us about workers in supported housing units who made time for them and helped them with many different aspects of their lives. There were examples of foster carers who were prepared to waive some of the procedural boundaries imposed on young parents through social care structures in order to enhance their sense of well-being. Young people particularly valued such services – and the professionals who provided them – so much more than those services and professionals they had encountered in other settings, which tended to work with them in more punitive and controlling ways.

Throughout this book, we have sought to balance the somewhat negative experiences of young parents from care with those that are more positive, even optimistic, in nature. We do not think that recent policies and programmes alone can provide simple solutions to the challenging circumstances in which young parents from care are too regularly placed. However, if properly resourced, there are new opportunities for professionals to listen and learn from young people and to work with them in ways which are likely to keep them engaged with, and able to fully benefit from, available services. Working in this way, professionals can build on their own as well as young people's strengths to develop further and to consolidate much of the good work currently taking place with young parents in and from care.

REFERENCES

Abrams, M. (1959) *The Teenage Consumer*, LPE Paper 5. London: London Press Exchange.

Acheson, D. (1998) *Independent Inquiry into Inequalities in Health Report.* London: The Stationery Office.

Aggleton, P., Oliver, C. and Rivers, K. (1998) *Reducing the Rate of Teenage Conceptions: The Implications of Research into Young People, Sex, Sexuality and Relationships.* London: Health Education Authority.

Alan Guttmacher Institute (1998) *Into a New World: Young Women's Sexual and Reproductive Lives.* New York: Alan Guttmacher Institute.

Allen, I. and Bourke Dowling, S. (1998) *Teenage Mothers: Decisions and Outcomes.* London: Policy Studies Institute.

Arai, L. (2003) 'Low expectations, sexual attitudes and knowledge: explaining teenage pregnancy and fertility in English communities. Insights from qualitative research.' *Sociological Review 51,* 2, 199–217.

Arcelus, J., Bellerby, T. and Vostanis, P. (1999) 'A mental health service for young people in the care of the local authority.' *Clinical Child Psychology and Psychiatry 4,* 2, 233–45.

Barn, R. and Mantovani, N. (2007) 'Young mothers and the care system: contextualising risk and vulnerability.' *British Journal of Social Work 37,* 2, 225–43.

BBC News Online. (2000)'Pupils pregnant for a day.'31 January. Available at news.bbc.co.uk/1/low/wales/624960.stm, accessed on 5 April 2008.

Bhabra, S., Ghate, D. and Brazier, L. (2002) *Consultation Analysis: Raising the Educational Attainment of Children in Care.* London: Policy Research Bureau.

Biehal, N., Clayden, J., Stein, M. and Wade, J. (1995) *Moving On: Young People and Leaving Care Schemes.* London: HMSO.

Blake, S. and Francis, G. (2001) *Just Say NO! – to Abstinence Education: Lessons Learnt from a Sex Education Study Tour to the United States.* London: Sex Education Forum and National Children's Bureau.

Bottrell, D. (2007) 'Resistance, resilience and social identities: reframing "problem youth" and the problem of schooling.' *Journal of Youth Studies 10,* 5, 597–616.

Bradshaw, J. (2006) *Teenage Births.* York: Joseph Rowntree Foundation.

Brake, M. (1985) *Comparative Youth Culture.* London: Routledge and Kegan Paul.

Broad, B. (2005) *Improving the Health and Well-Being of Young People Leaving Care.* London: Russell House.

Brodie, I., Berridge, D. and Beckett, W. (1997) 'The health of children looked after by local authorities.' *British Journal of Nursing 6,* 7, 386–91.

Buchanan, A. (1999) 'Are care leavers significantly dissatisfied and depressed in adult life?' *Adoption and Fostering 23,* 4, 35–40.

Burghes, L. and Brown, M. (1995) *Single Lone Mothers: Problems Prospects and Policies.* London: Families Policy Studies Centre.

Burtney, E. (2000) *Evidence into Actions: Teenage Sexuality in Scotland.* Edinburgh: Health Education Board for Scotland.

Buston, K. and Wight, D. (2002) 'The salience and utility of school sex education to young women.' *Sex Education 2,* 3, 233–50.

Buston, K. and Wight, D. (2006) 'The salience and utility of school sex education to young men.' *Sex Education 6,* 2, 135–50.

Carabine, J. (1996) 'Heterosexuality and Social Policy.' In D. Richardson (ed.) *Theorising Heterosexuality.* Buckingham: Open University Press.

Card, J. (1999) 'Teen pregnancy prevention: do any programs work?' *Annual Review of Public Health 20,* 257–85.

Centrepoint (2006) *Care Leavers: A Place to Call Home. Care Leavers' Experience of Finding Suitable Accommodation.* London: Centrepoint.

Chambers, R., Wakley, G. and Chambers, S. (2001) *Tackling Teenage Pregnancy: Sex, Culture and Needs.* Abingdon: Radcliffe Medical Press.

Chase, E., Simon, A. and Jackson, S. (eds) (2006) *In Care and After: A Positive Perspective.* London: Routledge.

Cheesbrough, S., Ingham, R. and Massey, D. (1999) *Summary Bulletin: Reducing the Rate of Teenage Conceptions. An International Review of the Evidence: USA, Canada, Australia and New Zealand.* London: Health Education Authority.

ChildLine (2007) *A ChildLine Information Sheet: Children in Care.* London: National Society for the Prevention of Cruelty to Children.

Collins, C., Alagiri, P., Summer, I. and Morin, S.F. (2002) *Abstinence Only vs. Comprehensive Sex Education. What are the Arguments? What is the Evidence?* San Francisco, CA: AIDS Policy Research Center and Center for AIDS Prevention Studies.

Corlyon, J. and McGuire, C. (1997) *Young Parents in Public Care: Pregnancy and Parenthood among Young People Looked After by Local Authorities.* London: National Children's Bureau.

Corlyon, J. and McGuire, C. (1999) *Pregnancy and Parenthood: The Views and Experiences of Young People in Public Care.* London: National Children's Bureau.

Cragg Ross Dawson Ltd (1999) *Summary Bulletin: Reducing the Rate of Teenage Conceptions.* London: Health Education Authority.

Daguerre, A. (2006) 'Teenage Pregnancy and Parenthood in England.' In A. Daguerre and C. Nativel (eds) *When Children Become Parents: Welfare State Responses to Teenage Pregnancy.* Bristol: Policy Press.

Daguerre, A. and Nativel, C. (eds) (2006) *When Children Become Parents: Welfare State Responses to Teenage Pregnancy.* Bristol: Policy Press.

Daves, J.A. (1995) 'Addressing television sexuality with adolescents.' *Pediatric Annals 24*, 79–82.

Davis, J. (1990) *Youth and the Condition of Britain.* London: Athlone.

Davis, M. (2001) 'Young black fathers.' *Young People's Health Network Newsletter 15*, 14, 48–50.

Dearden, K.A., Hale, C.B. and Woolley, T. (1995) 'The antecedents of teen fatherhood: a retrospective case-control study of Great Britain youth.' *American Journal of Public Health 85*, 551–54.

Department for Children, Schools and Families (DCSF) (2007a) *Children Looked After in England (Including Adoption and Care Leavers) Year Ending 31 March 2007.* Available at www.dcsf.gov.uk/rsgateway/DB/SFR/s000741/index.shtml, accessed on 7 May 2008.

Department for Children, Schools and Families (DCSF) (2007b) *Children's Plan: Building Brighter Futures.* London: DCSF.

Department for Children, Schools and Families (DCSF) (2007c) *Care Matters: Time for Change.* London: DCSF.

Department for Children, Schools and Families (DCSF) (2008) *Care Matters: Time to Deliver for Children in Care. An Implementation Plan.* London: DCSF.

Department for Education and Employment (DfEE) (2000) *Sex and Relationship Education Guidance.* Nottingham: DfEE.

Department for Education and Skills (DfES) (2004) *Every Child Matters: Change for Children.* London: DfES.

Department for Education and Skills (DfES) (2005a) *Government Response to Third Annual Report of the Independent Advisery Group on Teenage Pregnancy.* London: Teenage Pregnancy Unit.

Department for Education and Skills (DfES) (2005b) *Youth Matters.* Norwich: HMSO.

Department for Education and Skills (DfES) (2006a) *Teenage Pregnancy: Accelerating the Strategy to 2010.* Nottingham: DfES.

Department for Education and Skills (DfES) (2006b) *Care Matters: Transforming the Lives of Children and Young People in Care.* London: The Stationery Office.

Department for Education and Skills (DfES) (2007) *Care Matters: Time for Change.* London: The Stationery Office.

Department of Health (DH) (1998) *The Quality Protects Programme: Transforming Children's Services*, LAC (98) 28. London: DH.

Department of Health (DH) (1999) *Promoting Health for Looked After Children.* London: DH.

Department of Health (DH) (2000) *Guidance on the Education of Children and Young People in Public Care.* London: DfEE and DH.

Department of Health (DH) (2001a) *The National Strategy for Sexual Health and HIV.* London: DH.

Department of Health (DH) (2001b) *The Children Act Report 2000.* London: DH.

Department of Health (DH) (2002) *Promoting the Health of Looked After Children.* London: DH.

Department of Health (DH) (2004) *The National Service Framework for Children, Young People and Maternity Services.* London: DH.

Department of Health (DH) (2007) *Teenage Pregnancy Research Programme Research Briefing: Consequences of Teenage Parenthood. Pathways which Minimise the Long Term Negative Impacts of Teenage Childbearing.* London: DH.

Duncan, S. (2007) 'What's the problem with teenage parents? And what's the problem with policy?' *Critical Social Policy 27*, 3, 307–34.

European Commission (2000) *Report of the State of Young People's Health in the European Union.* Helsinki: European Commission.

France, A. (2007) *Understanding Youth in Late Modernity.* Maidenhead: Open University Press.

Gilligan, R. (2000) 'Adversity, resilience and young people: the protective value of positive school and spare time experiences' *Children and Society 14,* 1, 37–47.

Gilligan, R. (2001) *Promoting Resilience: A Resource Guide on Working with Children in the Care System.* London: British Agencies for Adoption and Fostering.

Gilligan, R. (2004) 'Promoting resilience in child and family social work: issues for social work practice, education and policy.' *Social Work Education 23,* 1, 93–104.

Gilroy, P. (1987) *There Ain't No Black in the Union Jack.* London: Routledge.

Hall, G.S. (1904) *Adolescence: Its Psychology and its Relations to Physiology, Anthropology, Sociology, Sex, Crime, Religion and Education.* New York: Appleton.

Hanna, B. (2001) 'Adolescent parenthood: a costly mistake or a search for love.' *Reproductive Health Matters 9,* 101–5.

Health Development Agency (2001) *Teenage Pregnancy: An Update on Key Characteristics of Effective Interventions.* London: Health Development Agency.

HM Treasury and DCSF (2007) *Aiming High for Young People: A Ten Year Strategy for Positive Activities.* London: HM Treasury.

Hoffman, L., Thornton, A. and Manis, J. (1978) 'The value of children to parents in the United States.' *Journal of Population 1,* 91–131.

Holland, J. Reynolds, T. and Weller, S. (2007) 'Transitions, networks and communities: the significance of social capital in the lives of children and young people.' *Journal of Youth Studies 10,* 1, 97–116.

Home Office (2004) *Delinquent Youth Groups and Offending Behaviour: Findings from the 2004 Offending, Crime and Justice Survey.* London: Home Office. Available at www.homeoffice.gov.uk/rds/pdfs06/rdsolr1406.pdf, accessed on 19 June 2008.

House of Commons Health Committee (2003) *The Victoria Climbé Inquiry Report (The Laming Report).* London: The Stationery Office.

Jackson, S. and Martin, P.Y. (1998) 'Surviving the care system: education and resilience.' *Journal of Adolescence 21,* 569–83.

Jackson, S., Ajayi, S. and Quigley, M. (2003) *By Degrees: The First Year. From Care to University.* London: National Children's Bureau and Frank Buttle Trust.

Kalmuss, D., Brickner, N. and Cushman, L.F. (1991) 'Adoption versus parenting among young pregnant women.' *Family Planning Perspectives 23,* 17–23.

Keirnan, K.E. (1995) *Transition to Parenthood: Young Mothers, Young Fathers – Associated Factors and Later Life Experiences.* London: London School of Economics.

Kirby, D. (1999) 'Sexuality and sex education at home and school.' *Adolescent Medicine: State of the Art Review 10,* 2, 195–209.

Kirby, D., Laris, B. and Rolleri, L. (2007) 'Sex and HIV education programs: their impact on sexual behaviors of young people throughout the world.' *Journal of Adolescent Health 40,* 3, 206–17.

Knight, A., Chase, E. and Aggleton, P. (2006) 'Someone of our own to love: experiences of being looked after as influences on teenage pregnancy.' *Children and Society 20,* 5, 391–403.

Krishnamoorthy, N., Simpson, C., Townend, J., Helms, P. and McLay, J. (2008) 'Adolescent females and hormonal contraception: a retrospective study in primary care.' *Journal of Adolescent Health 42*, 1, 97–101.

Lee, E., Clements, S., Ingham, R. and Stone, N. (2004) *A Matter of Choice? Explaining National Variation in Teenage Abortion and Motherhood.* York: Joseph Rowntree Foundation.

Lindsay, J., Smith, A.M.A. and Rosenthal, D.A. (1999) 'Conflicting advice? Australian adolescents use of condoms or the pill.' *Family Planning Perspectives 31*, 190–4.

Macleod, M. (1997) *Child Protection: Everybody's Business.* London: ChildLine.

Meltzer, H., Gatward, R., Corbin, T., Goodman, R. and Ford, T. (2003) *The Mental Health of Young People Looked After by Local Authorities in England.* London: The Stationery Office.

Michaels, G. and Brown, R. (1987) 'Values of children in adolescent mothers.' Unpublished paper.

Miller, J.W., Naimi, T.S., Brewer, R.D., Jones, S.E. (2007) 'Binge drinking and associated health risk behaviors among high school students.' *Pediatrics 119*, 76–85.

Morris, S. and Wheatley, H. (1994) *Time to Listen: The Experiences of Young People in Foster and Residential Care.* London: ChildLine.

Mueller, T., Gavin, L. and Kulkarni, A. (2008) 'The association between sex education and youth's engagement in sexual intercourse, age at first intercourse, and birth control use at first sex.' *Journal of Adolescent Health 42*, 1, 89–96.

Musick, J.S. (1993) *Young, Poor and Pregnant: The Psychology of Teenage Motherhood.* New Haven, CT: Yale University Press.

National Children's Homes (2007) *Literature Review: Resilience in Children and Young People.* London: NCH.

National Foster Care Association (NFCA) (1997) *Foster Care in Crisis.* London: NFCA.

NHS Centre for Reviews and Dissemination (1997) 'Preventing and reducing the adverse effects of unintended teenage pregnancies.' *Effective Health Care Bulletin 3*, 1–12.

O'Dougherty Wright, M. and Marsten, A. (2006) 'Resilience Processes in Development: Fostering Positive Adaptation in the Context of Adversity.' In S. Goldstein and R. Brooks (eds) *Handbook of Resilience in Children.* New York: Springer.

Office of the Deputy Prime Minister (ODPM) (2003) *Supporting People Strategy.* London: ODPM. Available at www.spkweb.org.uk, accessed on 19 June 2008.

Ofsted (2007a) *Children's Messages on Care: A Report by the Children's Rights Director for England.* London: HMSO.

Ofsted (2007b) *Children on Care Standards: Children's Views on National Minimum Standards for Children's Social Care. A Report by the Children's Rights Director for England.* London: HMSO.

Phoenix, A. (1991) *Young Mothers?* Cambridge: Polity Press.

Pollock, S. (2001) 'Young first time fathers: influences on commitment.' *Young People's Health Network Newsletter 15*, 8, 26–8. Available at www.nice.org.uk/nicemedia/documents/yphn_15.pdf, accessed on 19 June 2008

Quinton, D., Pollock, S. and Golding, J. (2002) *The Transition to Fatherhood by Young Men: Influences on Commitment.* London: Economic and Social Research Council. Available at www.esrc.ac.uk/mueyb%2fD0VWFA8kV8I44iKdc1SKu3ii1edxhBrnc8W4r%2fFzjUbu M6fRcj5Mp%2f9&xu=0&isAwardHolder=&isProfiled=&AwardHolderID=&Sector=, accessed on 19 June 2008.

Ray, C. (1998) *Highlight: Sex Education*. London: National Children's Bureau and Barnardo's.

Richardson, J. and Joughin, C. (2000) *Mental Health Needs of Looked After Children*. London: Gaskell.

Royal College of General Practitioners (RCGP) and Brook (2001) *Confidentiality and Young People: Improving Teenagers' Uptake of Sexual and Other Health Advice. A Toolkit for General Practice, Primary Care Groups and Trusts*. London: RCGP.

Rutman, D., Strega, S., Callahan, M. and Dominelli, L. (2002) '"Undeserving" mothers? Practitioners' experiences working with young mothers in/from care.' *Child and Family Social Work 7*, 3, 149–59.

Rutter, M. (1999) 'Resilience concepts and findings: implications for family therapy.' *Journal of Family Therapy 21*, 119–44.

Saleeby, D. (1996) 'The strengths perspective in social work practice.' *Social Work Education 41*, 3, 296–305.

Sawtell, M., Wiggins, M., Austerberry, H., Rosato, M., and Oliver, S. (2005) *Reaching Out to Pregnant Teenagers and Teenage Parents: Innovative Practice from Sure Start Plus Programmes*. London: Social Science Research Unit, Institute of Education, University of London.

Schoon, I. and Bynner, J. (2003) 'Risk and resilience in the life course: implications for interventions and social policies.' *Journal of Youth Studies 6*, 1, 21–31.

Scottish Executive (2000) *Report of the Scottish Youth Summit*. Edinburgh: Scottish Executive.

Shaw, C. (1998) *Remember My Messages... The Experiences and Views of 2000 Children in the UK*. London: The Who Cares? Trust.

Smith, T. (1993) 'Influence of socioeconomic factors on attaining targets for reducing teenage pregnancies.' *British Medical Journal 306*, 1232–35.

Social Exclusion Unit (1999a) *Teenage Pregnancy*. London: HMSO.

Social Exclusion Unit (1999b) *Bridging the Gap: New Opportunities for 16–18-Year-Olds Not in Education, Employment or Training*. London: HMSO.

Social Exclusion Unit (2003) *A Better Education for Children in Care: Social Exclusion Unit Report*. London: Social Exclusion Unit, Office of the Deputy Prime Minister.

Social Services Inspectorate (2001) *Developing Quality to Protect Children: SSI Inspection of Children's Services August 1999–July 2000*. London: Department of Health.

Speak, S., Cameron, S. and Gilroy, R. (1997) *Young Single Fathers: Participation in Fatherhood – Barriers and Bridges*. London: Family Policy Studies Centre.

Stein, M. (2002) 'Leaving Care.' In D. McNeish, T. Newman and H. Roberts (eds) *What Works for Children*. Oxford: Oxford University Press.

Stein, M. (2005) *Resilience and Young People Leaving Care: A Literature Review Exploring the Factors Affecting Young People Leaving Care as they Move into Adulthood and Independency*. York: Joseph Rowntree Foundation.

Swann, C., Bowe, K., McCormick, G. and Kosmin, M. (2003) *Teenage Pregnancy and Parenthood: a Review of Reviews*. London: Health Development Agency.

Szmigin, I., Griffin, C., Hackley, C., Bengry-Howell, A.,Weale, L. and Mistral, W. (2008) 'Reframing "binge drinking" as calculated hedonism: empirical evidence from the UK.' *International Journal of Drug Policy, 19*, 5, 359–66.

Tabberer, S., Hall, C., Prendergast, S. and Webster, A. (2000) *Teenage Pregnancy and Choice: Abortion or Motherhood: Influences on the Decision*. York: Joseph Rowntree Foundation.

Teenage Pregnancy Unit (2000) *Best Practice Guidance on the Provision of Effective Contraceptive and Advice Services for Young People.* London: Teenage Pregnancy Unit.

Teenage Pregnancy Unit (2001) *Guidance for Developing Contraception and Sexual Health Advice Services to Reach Boys and Young Men.* London: Teenage Pregnancy Unit.

Turner, K.M. (2004) 'Young women's views on teenage motherhood: a possible explanation for the relationship between socio-economic background and teenage pregnancy outcome?' *Journal of Youth Studies* 7, 2, 221–38.

Tyrer, P., Chase, E., Warwick, I. and Aggleton, P. (2005) 'Dealing with it: experiences of young fathers in and leaving care.' *British Journal of Social Work 35*, 1–15.

UNICEF (2001) *A League Table of Teenage Births in Rich Nations.* Innocenti Report, 3. Florence: Innocenti Research Centre.

Wade, J., Biehal, N., Clayden, J. and Stein, M. (1998) *Going Missing: Young People Absent from Care.* Chichester: Wiley.

Ward, H. and Skuse, T. (2001) 'Looking after children: using data as management information. Report from the first year of data collection.' Unpublished paper.

Ward, L. (2008) 'Binge drinking fuels youth violence.' *Guardian*, 23 January. Available at www.guardian.co.uk/society/2008/jan/23/youngdrinkers, accessed on 11 June 2008.

Weick, A. and Saleeby, D. (1995) 'Supporting family strengths: orienting policy and practice toward the 21st century.' *Families in Society 76*, 3, 141.

Wellings, K., Wadsworth, J., Johnson, A., Field, J., Whitaker, L. and Field, B. (1995) 'Provision of sex education and early sexual experience: the relation examined.' *British Medical Journal 311*, 417–20.

Wellings, K., Nanchahal, K., Macdowall, W., McManus, S., *et al.* (2001) 'Sexual behaviour in Britain: early heterosexual experience.' *Lancet 358*, 1843–50.

Wight, D., Henderson, M., Raab, G.M., Abraham, C. *et al.* (2000) 'Extent of regretted sexual intercourse among teenagers in Scotland: a cross-sectional survey.' *British Medical Journal*, *320* 1243–4.

Wight, D., Raab, G.M., Henderson, M., Abraham, C. *et al.* (2002) 'Limits of teacher delivered sex education: interim behavioural outcomes from randomised trial.' *British Medical Journal 324*, 1430–3.

Young, E. (2008) 'It's not fair: brains may compel teens to tantrum.' *New Scientist* 25 February. Available at www.newscientist.com/channel/being-human/dn13373-its-not-fair-brains-may-compel-teens-to-tantrum.html, accessed on 11 June 2008.

ACTS OF PARLIAMENT

Care Standards Act 2000. London: Office of Public Sector Information. Available at www.opsi.gov.uk/acts/acts2000/ukpga_20000014_en_1, accessed on 19 June 2008.

Children Act 1989. London: Office of Public Sector Information. Available at www.opsi.gov.uk/acts/acts1989/ukpga_19890041_en_1, accessed on 19 June 2008.

Children Act 2004. London: Office of Public Sector Information. Available at www.opsi.gov.uk/acts/acts2004/ukpga_20040031_en_1, accessed on 19 June 2008.

Children (Leaving Care) Act 2000. London: Office of Public Sector Information. Available at www.opsi.gov.uk/acts/acts2000/ukpga_20000035_en_1, accessed on 19 June 2008.

SUBJECT INDEX

Page numbers in *italics* refer to tables

abandonment 55, 59, 61, 69, 96, 100
abortions 21–2, 27–8, 39, 59, 90, 95–9, 100
   pressure to terminate 93–4
absconding *see* running away
abuse 24, 25, 55, 57, 58, 63, 64, 69, 171
   sexual abuse 62, 63
   see also violence
accommodation 10, 26, 43, 49, 94, 108, 111, 113, 151, 154, 155, 166, 171, 173
   bed and breakfast 43, 49, 112, 152
   temporary accommodation 109, 112, 118, 119, 135, 152, 153, 163
achievement 98–9
adoption 21, 96–9, 100
   removal of babies for adoption 143, 144, 145
affection 100
Aiming High for Young People: A Ten Year Strategy for Positive Activities (HM Treasury and DCSF) 175

alcohol abuse 14, 18, 37, 48, 49, 81, 102, 116, 118, 122, 124, 128, 168, 171
amphetamines 118, 126
antenatal care 23, 28, 40, 44, 104–8
antisocial behaviour 15
asylum seekers 24
attention deficit hyperactivity disorder (ADHD) 76, 142, 143

behavioural problems 15, 45, 143
benefits 13, 22, 26, 151, 159, 165–6
Better Education of Children in Care (Social Exclusion Unit) 28
birth 31
bullying 25

cannabis 50, 118, 122, 126
care 16, 28, 30, 69
   continuity of care 173–4
   feelings about being in care 65–6
   lives before care 56–9
   multiple placements 64
Care Matters: Time for Change (Department for Education and Skills (DfES)) 15, 29–30, 172

Care Matters: Transforming the Lives of Children and Young People (Department for Education and Skills (DfES)) 15, 29–30, 174
Care Standards Act 2000 28
Care2learn 172
Change for Children 172
child protection assessments 138, 149–50, 170
   young people's perspectives 138–43
childcare 17, 151, 162–4
Children Act 1989 25
Children Act 2004 15
Children (Leaving Care) Act 2000 15, 25, 28, 29, 30, 156
Children's Plan: Building Brighter Futures (Department for Children, Schools and Families (DCSF)) 15, 16
Climbié, Victoria 148
confidentiality 76
Connexions 33
contraception 16, 17, 27, 30, 41, 51, 84
   ignorance of 72, 73–4, 75
   involuntary 38–9
   pregnancy 85, 86
   young people 20–1, 77–9, 100, 101

control 98, 99
crack cocaine 118, 119, 120
crèches 163, 165
crime 14, 81
cultural factors 14, 37, 100
    immigrant children 56–7,
    58

Denmark 20
depression 22, 142
    post-natal depression 38,
    52, 53, 110, 126–7,
    137, 162, 169
disabilities 10, 39, 40, 54
dope see cannabis
drug abuse 10, 18, 37, 38,
    42, 81, 102, 106, 122,
    124, 125–6, 152, 168,
    171
    pregnancy 118–20
    removal of children into
    care 47–9, 126,
    139–40, 146
    residential care 60
dyslexia 49, 143

economic disadvantage 15
ecstasy 118
education 16, 17, 22, 23, 28,
    37, 137, 151, 164–6
    during pregnancy 115–16
    looked after children
    25–6, 28–9, 172
    young people's
    experiences 67–8
    young people's plans
    40–1, 45, 53
educational support workers
    36, 144
emergency hormonal
    contraception 20–1
emotional factors 100–1
empathy bellies 75
employment 16, 17, 22, 23,
    26, 28, 29, 151, 164,
    165

England 15, 31–2, 35, 56,
    58, 82, 112, 124
    abortions 21
    looked after children 24,
    172
    sex education 19
    teenage conceptions 16,
    17, 20, 171
ethnicity 10, 14, 24–5, 29,
    36, 37
Europe 21
Every Child Matters
    (Department for
    Education and Skills
    (DfES)) 15, 173–4
exploitation 46, 60, 113,
    168

families 10, 55, 59, 65, 69,
    130–4
family support workers 36,
    43, 81, 140
fathers 9, 13, 22, 23, 31,
    122, 124–6, 137
focus 98, 171
foster care 25, 36, 38, 41–2,
    45, 49–50, 55–6, 151
    mother and baby
    placements 159–61
    pregnancy 92–3, 111
    sex education 74, 82–3,
    84
    young people's opinions
    61–3, 177
friends 134–5

general practitioners (GPs)
    40, 41, 52, 78, 93, 127,
    142, 162
    pregnancy 105, 107, 108
grants 151, 165–6
Guidance on the Education of
    Children and Young People
    in Public Care
    (Department of Health
    (DH)) 28

health services 15, 16, 44,
    137, 151, 170
health visitors 40, 44,
    106–7, 108, 141, 162
heroin 10, 47–9, 54, 63
heterosexuality 14
HIV 75
homelessness 23, 26, 38, 42,
    51, 82, 112–14, 119,
    141, 171
hostels 113, 115, 116, 119,
    152, 153, 155
housing 13, 14, 16, 17, 22,
    112–15, 137, 151–5,
    159, 170, 171
    housing support workers
    132, 177
    supported housing units
    36, 77, 135, 153–4,
    177

identity 98
insecurity 56, 113, 168
instability 64, 69, 98
    residential care 81
isolation 61, 154

Laming Report 148
law-breaking 22
learning difficulties 45, 84,
    143, 145, 147–8
leaving care services 151,
    156–9, 170
leaving care workers 36, 40,
    44, 54, 73, 110, 113,
    114, 134, 166
    child protection
    assessments 144–5,
    145–6
    professionals' perspectives
    79–80
    young people's opinions
    156–9, 176–7
local authorities 9, 15, 35
loneliness 27, 98
looked after children 9–10,
    11, 55–6, 172

early pregnancy 27–8
education 25–6, 28–9,
     172
health and well-being
     24–6
improving support for
     28–31
opinions of children in
     care 30
love 100

menstruation 38, 43, 47, 72,
     75, 83, 86
mental health problems 18,
     26, 29
midwifery services 33, 36,
     40, 44, 45, 49
     specialist teenage
          pregnancy midwives
          105–6, 107–8, 154,
          169, 177
miscarriages 47
mothers 9, 13, 14, 23–4, 31
     mother and baby units
          112, 114, 135, 153,
          154

National Minimum Standards
     for social care 30
National Service Framework for
     Children, Young People and
     Maternity Services
     (Department of Health
     (DH)) 15–16, 28
National Teenage Pregnancy
     Strategy (Social Exclusion
     Unit) 15, 16–17
neglect 24, 171
Nigeria 56, 58
Norway 20
nurseries 135, 163, 165
nurses
     community 40
     school-based 20
     specialist 36, 82, 93

offending behaviour 15, 14,
     22, 81
     young offenders 46, 117,
          122, 123, 137
     youth offending teams 33,
          36, 115

parenthood 9, 10–11, 28,
     30, 31, 84, 136–7, 169,
     170–1
     feelings about prospect of
          parenthood 103–4
     new responsibilities, new
          challenges 123–6
     positive aspects 23, 38,
          50–1, 135–6
     time of change 122–3
     young people 22–4, 69,
          121–2
partners 89–90, 128–30
peer pressure 27, 37
policy considerations 170–2
pornography 71
post-natal depression 38, 52,
     53, 110, 126–7, 137,
     162, 169
poverty 23
pregnancy 9, 10, 19, 30, 31,
     37–8, 68, 69, 84, 102,
     120, 169
     deciding what to do 92–5
     drug abuse 118–20
     education during
          pregnancy 115–16
     feelings about pregnancy
          103–4
     health risks 22
     looked after children
          27–8
     reactions of partners
          89–90
     reactions of relatives 90–2
     relationships during
          pregnancy 116–18
     social services 108–11,
          117–18

teenage conceptions 16,
     17, 20, 171
     young people's responses
          85–9, 99–101
Pregnancy and Parenthood
     Among Young People In
     and Leaving Local
     Authority Care 31–3
     Age of young men at
          interview and at first
          becoming parents 34
     Age of young women at
          interview and at first
          becoming parents 34
     research participants 33–6
primary care services 15,
     151, 162
probation teams 33
professional practice 173–7
     adequate resourcing 174
     continuity of care 173–4
     listening to young people
          174–5
     promoting young people's
          strengths 175–7
     transparency 173
professionals' perspectives
     79–84, 99, 112, 133,
     169
     child protection
          assessments 143–9
     project development workers
          146–7
Promoting Health for Looked
     After Children
     (Department of Health
     (DH)) 28
prostitution 26
protective factors 14
purpose 98

Quality Protects Programme
     (Department of Health
     (DH)) 28

racism 63
rape 49, 119

rejection 55, 56, 59, 61, 65, 69, 96, 100, 168, 171
relationships 9, 10, 17, 19, 20, 26, 29, 31, 42, 69, 101, 168–9
    exploitative relationships 46, 60
    learning about sex 73–7
    pregnancy 86
    relationships during pregnancy 116–18
    relationships with family 55, 59, 65, 69, 130–4
    relationships with friends 134–5
    relationships with parents 52–3, 57–9
    relationships with partners 128–30
    relationships with residential care staff 59–60
residential care 25, 36, 45–6, 50, 55
    instability 81
    pregnancy 111
    young people's opinions 59–61
resilience 14, 175
responsibility 10, 14, 53, 54
    parenthood 123–6
running away 25, 41–2, 60, 63

schools 74, 75, 171
    school exclusion 25, 38, 67, 68, 165
    school counsellors 115–16
    school-based nurses 20
Scotland 22
security 10, 98, 173, 174
self-harming 26
sex 69, 70, 84, 168
    learning about sex 73–7

young people's uncertainties 71–3
sex education 10, 17, 19–20, 27, 29, 30, 31, 74–5, 83–4, 101, 168–9
    foster care 74, 82–3
    lack of 42–3, 71–3
    professionals' perspectives 80
    young people's opinions 74–6
sexual abuse 62, 63
sexual behaviour 26
sexual health services 76–7, 79–80
sexual initiation 10, 18, 27, 38, 46, 71
Sierra Leone 57
single mothers' hostels 115

social factors 14–15, 100
social services 28, 32, 83, 137, 138–9, 151, 170
    opinions of young people 44, 48–9, 62, 155–6
    pregnancy 108–11, 117–18
social workers 30, 36, 39, 44, 62, 70, 80, 81, 82, 93, 102, 117, 174
    child protection assessments 138, 139, 141–2, 145
    professionals' perspectives 99, 112, 143, 144, 146, 147–8
    young people's experiences 66–7, 73, 106, 110–11, 134, 166
socio-economic deprivation 21–2, 23
speed see amphetamines
stability 10, 54, 171, 173, 174
STIs (sexually transmitted infections) 75

suicide 26
support services 16, 17, 23, 26, 28, 151, 166, 170
    adequate resourcing 174
Supporting People Strategy (Office of the Deputy Prime Minister (ODPM)) 171
Sure Start Plus 33, 36, 93, 99, 106, 154, 165, 183
Sweden 20

teachers 19, 68, 70, 76, 116, 184
teenage conceptions 16, 17, 20, 171
teenage pregnancy coordinators 17, 32, 36, 123, 144, 162, 164
Teenage Pregnancy: Accelerating the Strategy to 2010 (Department for Education and Skills (DfES)) 15, 16
teenagers 9, 13
Thomas Coram Research Unit, University of London 31
training 16, 17, 29, 164
transparency 173
truancy 22, 60

UK 14, 20, 30, 36, 55, 56, 57, 172
unemployment 14, 26
University of London 31
USA 20

violence 10, 14, 38, 49, 51, 55, 58, 69, 119, 120, 127–8, 137, 141, 168, 171
    child protection assessments 145
    reactions to pregnancy 89–90

violence during pregnancy
116–17
violence *see also* abuse
voluntary sector 32, 33, 36,
80, 158, 164–5

welfare benefits *see* benefits
well-being 15, 16, 23, 24–6
work opportunities 17

young offenders 46, 117,
122, 123, 137
young people 9, 10, 11,
13–16, 55–6
abortions 21–2, 27–8,
95–9, 100
adoption 96–9, 100
child protection
assessments 138–43
contraception 20–1,
77–9, 100, 101
learning about sex 73–7
listening to young people
174–5
need for support 167–70
parenthood 22–4, 69,
121–2
professionals' perspectives
79–84
promoting young people's
strengths 175–7
sexuality 18–20
uncertainties about sex
71–3
Youth Matters (Department for
Education and Skills
(DfES)) 15
youth offending teams 33,
36, 115

AUTHOR INDEX

Abrams, M. 13
Acheson, D. 17
Aggleton, P. 16, 24
Ajayi, S. 25
Alan Guttmacher Institute 16, 18
Allen, I. 21, 22
Arai, L. 23
Arcelus, J. 26

Barn, R. 23, 24, 28
BBC News Online 75
Beckett, W. 27
Bellerby, T. 26
Berridge, D. 27
Bhabra, S. 26
Biehal, N. 27
Blake, S. 19
Bottrell, D. 175
Bourke Dowling, S. 21, 22
Bradshaw, J. 16
Brake, M. 14
Brickner, N. 21
Broad, B. 26
Brodie, I. 27
Brook 21
Brown, M. 20, 21
Brown, R. 23
Buchanan, A. 26
Burghes, L. 20, 21
Burtney, E. 19
Buston, K. 19

Bynner, J. 14, 15

Cameron, S. 23
Carabine, J. 14
Card, J. 19
Centrepoint 26
Chambers, R.19, 23
Chambers, S. 19
Chase, E. 24, 26
Cheesbrough, S.16
ChildLine 25
Collins, C. 20
Corlyon, J. 24, 27, 28
Cragg Ross Dawson Ltd 22
Cushman, L.F. 21

Daguerre, A. 14, 17, 18, 20, 23
Daves, J.A. 19
Davis, J. 13
Davis, M. 23
Dearden, K.A. 22
Department for Children, Schools and Families (DCSF) 15, 16, 21, 24, 25, 27, 172, 174, 175
Department for Education and Employment (DfEE) 19
Department for Education and Skills (DfES) 15, 16, 17, 18, 27, 29, 30

Department of Health (DH) 15, 19, 22, 26, 28
Duncan, S. 27

European Commission 21

France, A. 14
Francis, G. 19

Gavin, L. 19
Gilligan, R. 14, 175, 176
Gilroy, P. 14
Gilroy, R. 23
Golding, J. 23

Hale, C.B. 22
Hall, G.S. 13
Hanna, B. 23
Health Development Agency 19
HM Treasury 175
Hoffman, L. 23
Holland, J. 175
Home Office 13
House of Commons Health Committee 148

Ingham, R. 16

Jackson, S. 25, 26
Joughin, C. 26

Kalmuss, D. 21
Keirnan, K.E. 20
Kirby, D. 19
Knight, A. 24
Krishnamoorthy, N. 21
Kulkarni, A. 19

Laris, B. 19
Lee, E. 21
Lindsay, J. 19, 20

Macleod, M. 25
Manis, J. 23
Mantovani, N. 23, 24, 28
Marsten, A. 14
Martin, P.Y. 26
Massey, D. 16
McGuire, C. 24, 27, 28
Meltzer, H. 29
Michaels, G. 23
Miller, J.W. 14
Morris, S. 25
Mueller, T. 19
Musick, J.S. 23

National Children's Homes
    14, 28
National Foster Care
    Association (NFCA) 28
Nativel, C. 14, 20, 23
NHS Centre for Reviews and
    Dissemination 23

O'Dougherty Wright, M. 14
Office of the Deputy Prime
    Minister (ODPM) 171
Ofsted 30
Oliver, C. 16

Phoenix, A. 23
Pollock, S. 22, 23

Quigley, M.25
Quinton, D. 23

Ray, C. 20

Reynolds, T. 175
Richardson, J. 26
Rivers, K. 16
Rolleri, L. 19
Rosenthal, D.A. 19
Royal College of General
    Practitioners (RCGP) 21
Rutman, D. 176
Rutter, M. 14

Saleeby, D. 175
Sawtell, M. 13
Schoon, I. 14, 15
Scottish Executive 19
Simon, A. 26
Skuse, T. 26
Smith, A.M.A. 19
Smith, T. 22
Social Exclusion Unit 15, 16,
    18, 20, 21, 22, 26, 28
Social Services Inspectorate
    26
Speak, S. 23
Stein, M. 26, 29
Swann, C. 27
Szmigin, I. 14

Tabberer, S. 22, 23
Teenage Pregnancy Unit 21
Thornton, A. 23
Turner, K.M. 22
Tyrer, P. 23

UNICEF 20

Vostanis, P. 26

Wade, J. 25
Wakley, G. 19
Ward, H. 26
Ward, L. 14
Weick, A. 175
Weller, S. 175
Wellings, K. 18, 19, 20
Wheatley, H. 25
Wight, D. 18, 19

Woolley, T. 22

Young, E. 13